DOUGLAS REEVES

FAST
Grading

A Guide to Implementing
Best Practices

Solution Tree | Press

a division of
Solution Tree

555 North Morton Street
Bloomington, IN 47404

800.733.6786 (toll free) / 812.336.7700
FAX: 812.336.7790

email: info@solution-tree.com
solution-tree.com

Visit **go.solution-tree.com/assessment** to download the free reproducibles in this book.

Printed in the United States of America

20   19   18   17   16   1   2   3   4   5

Library of Congress Cataloging-in-Publication Data

Names: Reeves, Douglas B., 1953- author.

Title: Fast grading : a guide to implementing best practices / Douglas Reeves.

Description: Bloomington, IN : Solution Tree Press, [2016] | Includes

   bibliographical references and index.

Identifiers: LCCN 2016003188 | ISBN 9781936763870 (perfect bound)

Subjects: LCSH: Grading and marking (Students)--Handbooks, manuals, etc.

Classification: LCC LB3060.37 .R44 2016 | DDC 371.27/2--dc23 LC record available at http://lccn.loc.gov/2016003188

Solution Tree
Jeffrey C. Jones, CEO
Edmund M. Ackerman, President

Solution Tree Press
President: Douglas M. Rife
Senior Acquisitions Editor: Amy Rubenstein
Editorial Director: Tonya Maddox Cupp
Managing Production Editor: Caroline Weiss
Senior Editor: Kari Gillesse
Proofreader: Evie Madsen
Compositor and Text Designer: Abigail Bowen
Cover Designers: Abigail Bowen and Rian Anderson

ACKNOWLEDGMENTS

The primary debt of authors is to our readers. Therefore, the most important acknowledgment is to the educators, administrators, and policymakers who are willing to grapple with the emotionally and politically challenging issue of grading. As you undertake this particularly challenging work, it's likely that few people have thanked you recently for your commitment, professionalism, and resilience. So if you haven't heard it lately, please hear it from me: thank you, thank you, thank you. As a parent and colleague, I truly appreciate your work.

Books never reach the hands of readers without an exceptional publishing team. In this, our seventh collaboration, I am indebted to Solution Tree Press President Douglas Rife, Solution Tree CEO Jeff Jones, Managing Production Editor Caroline Weiss, and Senior Editor Kari Gillesse.

Whenever students would tell me that they had an idea that was completely original, I knew that this was a not very clever way of telling me that they had not done their homework and considered their intellectual predecessors. My thinking on the subject of grading has been particularly influenced by Susan Brookhart, Tom Guskey, Bob Marzano, Ken O'Connor, and Rick Wormeli. Most important, I am indebted to the educators, parents, and administrators who have allowed me to collaborate with them to improve the quality of grading systems and ultimately, improve the effectiveness of teaching and learning in their schools.

Douglas Reeves
Boston, Massachusetts

Solution Tree Press would like to thank the following reviewers:

Kim Bailey
Past Director of Instructional
  Support and Professional
  Learning
Capistrano Unified School
  District
San Juan Capistrano, California

Beverly Clemens
Assistant Principal
Mesa Middle School
Castle Rock, Colorado

Hallie Edgerly
Science Teacher
Adel DeSoto Minburn Middle
  School
Adel, Iowa

Melissa Emler
Digital Leading and Learning
  Specialist
CESA 3
Fennimore, Wisconsin

Karrie Fansler
Instructional Literacy Coach
Evergreen Public Schools
Vancouver, Washington

Angela Freese
Director of Learning Analytics
  and Systems Improvement
Stillwater Public Schools
Stillwater, Minnesota

Michelle Goodwin
Associate Superintendent for
  Curriculum and Instruction
Montcalm Area School District
Stanton, Michigan
Ionia County Intermediate
  School District
Ionia, Michigan

Garnet Hillman
Instructional Coach
Caruso Middle School
Deerfield, Illinois

Jasmine Kullar
Principal
Northwestern Middle School
Milton, Georgia

Visit **go.solution-tree.com/assessment** to download
the free reproducibles in this book.

TABLE OF CONTENTS

PART I
BUILDING RELATIONSHIPS WITH TEACHERS, PARENTS, AND COMMUNITIES

PART II
IMPLEMENTING FAST GRADING AND IMPROVING BEST PRACTICES

PART III
CONSIDERING FAST FEEDBACK THROUGHOUT SCHOOLS, SYSTEMS, AND COMMUNITIES

ABOUT THE AUTHOR

 **Douglas Reeves, PhD**, is the author of more than thirty books and eighty articles about education, leadership, and organizational effectiveness. He has presented his work on effective grading practices to audiences around the world. His research appears in *Educational Leadership, Phi Delta Kappan, American School Board Journal*, and many other publications. His comments on grading appeared on the cover of *USA Today*, and his work remains frequently cited in professional and academic publications. Douglas's honors include the Distinguished Service Award from the National Association of Secondary School Principals, the Brock International Prize, and the Contribution to the Field Award from the National Staff Development Council (now Learning Forward). He is the founding editor and copublisher of *The SNAFU Review*, where he provides one-on-one support for disabled veterans whose writing and art inspire others with post-traumatic stress disorder. He is also the founder of Finish the Dissertation, a free and noncommercial service for doctoral students. He lives with his family in downtown Boston.

To learn more about Douglas's work, visit Creative Leadership Solutions (http://creativeleadership.net) or the *Change Leaders* blog (www.changeleaders.com), or follow him on Twitter @DouglasReeves.

To book Douglas Reeves for professional development, contact pd@solution-tree.com.

FAST GRADING: FAIR, ACCURATE, SPECIFIC, AND TIMELY

In the second edition of *Elements of Grading*, I advance four criteria for effective grading policies and practices (Reeves, 2016). Specifically, teachers, administrators, and educational systems must ensure that grading is fair, accurate, specific, and timely. *FAST Grading* provides practical steps for teachers to implement more effective grading policies in their classrooms. In conjunction with *Elements of Grading*, Second Edition, this book also provides educators with the basis for a constructive dialogue with parents and community members and the skills to develop effective grading practices.

It is essential to note at the outset that while FAST grading will save teachers time, it is not necessarily quick. Indeed, the provision of feedback that is fair, accurate, specific, and timely is a professionally mindful process that requires teachers and administrators to slow down in order to apply the FAST principles and, eventually, pick up the pace at which they deliver effective feedback. Moreover, I do not presume that readers of this volume are starting from scratch. In almost every school I have observed, there are teachers who are already experimenting with pilot projects or who have well-established grading reform policies, but they are operating independently, without much fanfare. Their effective practices are not yet expanded to schoolwide or districtwide policies. Therefore, one of the most important starting points for every discussion of grading practices is an inventory of great practices that are already in place. The best advocates for improved grading policies will be your colleagues who are already using them.

Why Grading Reform Is Worth the Effort

If I could offer a solution to readers that would, in less than a single year, reduce failure rates, improve discipline, and increase faculty morale, would it be worthy of consideration? Evidence overwhelmingly concludes that improved grading practices accomplish precisely those results. Thomas R. Guskey (2015), Douglas Reeves (2012), Jan Chappuis, Rick Stiggins, Steve Chappuis, and Judith Arter (2012), Ken O'Connor (2007), Robert J. Marzano (2006), and Thomas R. Guskey and Jane M. Bailey (2001) are just a few of the voices that use a variety of research techniques to demonstrate a common conclusion. When schools embrace effective grading practices and terminate toxic grading policies, student performance, motivation, and discipline improve. Not only do these solutions offer enormous advantages for students, schools, and teachers, but they also offer the promise of enduring impacts over time.

To examine the benefits of effective grading practices, let us consider the impact of the changes Cardinal Community School District in Iowa made to its grading policy in 2011. Superintendent Joel Pedersen's success is profiled in the *American School Board Journal* (Reeves, 2012). As the faculty at Cardinal Middle-Senior High School investigated the causes for student failures, it was clear that the most important cause was not a lack of student proficiency nor low scores on final examinations. It wasn't even class absences or disruptive behavior. The number one cause of student failure was missing homework. This is a refrain I have heard in schools around the world, where otherwise proficient students are failing classes because they have not completed homework assignments.

Pedersen and his colleagues decided that academic practice—just like athletic practice—had an important place in student proficiency. But they also observed that some students went home every night to an environment in which homework was emphasized and other students did not. Rather than continue to punish students through failures, the faculty decided to create a different opportunity for homework completion. They called it "The Ketchup Solution." The procedure was simple: from Monday through Thursday, the completion of homework was a matter strictly between the student and teacher. But students who had not completed homework by Thursday afternoon were assigned to the "Ketchup" room on Friday morning where they were expected to catch up on their homework. The time in the room might be only fifteen or twenty minutes, or it might be a couple of hours. The goal was to have every student in the school enter the weekend with homework completed and, most important, to avoid the end-of-semester disaster when passing the class became impossible for students who missed too many homework assignments.

What made Cardinal Community School District's policy particularly compelling is that there was no turnover in teachers and administrators and only a tiny amount of turnover among students, with intrayear mobility rates less than 10 percent. Thus, the changes in results that this system experienced had to be due almost entirely to the policy changes that the district made, including improved grading practices and alternative consequences for missing or poor student work. The results were astounding—more than a 95 percent reduction in student failures, a 55 percent reduction in suspensions, and a 2 percent increase in student attendance. Four years later, the district continued to make gains (J. Pedersen, personal communication, August 14, 2015). Because of Iowa's open enrollment laws, students and parents vote with their feet, sending students away from schools that are perceived as failing and toward schools that are perceived as successful. Before Pedersen and his colleagues began their improvements in grading practices, there was a net outflow of more than $300,000 each year as a result of the dollars following students to other districts. After four years of grading reform, there was more than an $880,000 inflow, a swing of more than $1 million (that is, from lost revenue of $300,000 to gained revenue of almost $900,000), and a major impact on the budget of this school system.

Moreover, these data indicate that parents appreciate and endorse improved grading practices. The problem facing teachers and educational leaders is this: if the case for grading reform is so obviously beneficial, why is it so difficult to implement?

Why Grading Reform Frequently Fails

I don't know of a single teacher, parent, board member, or community leader who actively seeks lower performance from schools and students. But I know many of them who defend toxic grading practices. Newspapers critical of schools join in the fray, chastising the advocates of grading reform for policies that, they declare, will undermine student work ethic and fail to recognize the work of the best students. Let us consider some of the specific issues that cause grading reform to go off the rails before it even begins.

Mistake 1: How *Before* Why

It's easy to see why school administrators are enthusiastic about implementing grading reforms. Who could possibly argue with increased achievement, better morale, and improved discipline? It turns out that lots of people do, not because grading reforms are ineffective, but because many skeptics have good reason to doubt the latest breathless claim from educational researchers. They have seen too many apparently good ideas implemented without results and, more often, purchased at great expense and then implemented poorly. For example, districts in the United States have invested billions of dollars in one-to-one computer initiatives, Smart Boards, and computerized testing programs. But the best evidence suggests that the most effective investment schools can make is in effective teaching (Hattie, 2012; Marzano, 2007). While I am not an educational Luddite suggesting that we destroy the machines lest they replace human workers, I am suggesting that ill-advised technology initiatives provide an important example of why teachers and parents are skeptical of new technological initiatives. I have personally observed computer screens freeze, causing students to wait as long as two hours to log on, and then spend as much as three and a half hours (at the elementary level!) taking tests. I've seen technology classrooms in which the Smart Boards and available technology sit idle as students, bored to tears, sit in row after row of desks while teachers present content in ways that are little different from half a century ago. These personal observations are consistent with large-scale quantitative studies I have conducted in which I found that the degree of implementation of educational initiatives was extremely low (Reeves, 2012). This leads skeptics of educational reform to rightly question, What did taxpayers and students actually get for all the money that was invested in these initiatives? Many educators can recall the various "reading wars" and "mathematics wars" in which ideology trumped a rational consideration of the evidence. No matter how obvious the evidence for improved grading may be, we must explain in clear and unmistakable terms why grading reform is good for students now and in the future.

Distinguishing between alternative educational reforms requires systematic comparison of schools with similar student demographic characteristics, teaching staff, and administrative policies, but only a few different instructional variables. In the best of circumstances, districts or other entities conducting research randomly assign schools and classrooms to a control group (without the intervention) or an experimental group (with the intervention). Then, with a sufficiently large sample size, researchers measure the differences between the two groups. This rarely occurs in educational research, in part because researchers are loath to randomly assign students to a group that deliberately omits a promising practice. It's the same ethical dilemma that medical researchers face when they randomly assign some cancer patients to receive the placebo, a drug that has no medicinal properties. Although this sort of randomized experiment is not available to most schools, it is certainly possible to replicate the Cardinal Community School District's practice of comparing the yearly results for students with nearly identical demographic characteristics in the same school with the same teachers and same curriculum and same financial constraints. One year, homework was a sink-or swim-affair and the next year they had the Ketchup Solution. These sorts of solid results allow teachers and other stakeholders to evaluate a proposed policy based upon the evidence, not based upon the promises of an enthusiastic salesperson. Schools can do similar experiments with a backward look at the data. For example, educators and administrators can simply look at the last semester of grades from students where the final grade was calculated based upon the average throughout the semester. They can then compare those results—failure rate and grade point averages—to the same students in the same classes if the teachers had the freedom to use other measurements, such as the latest and best evidence rather than the average. In other words, it doesn't take a federally funded study conducted by a university research department to reveal locally compelling research findings.

Mistake 2: Sympathy Over Rigor

Sometimes the rationale for improved grading practices appears to be a sympathetic attempt to help low-performing students. When, for example, new grading policies allow these students to retake exams, turn in homework late or not at all, or earn the same grade as a high-performing student, we should not expect teachers and parents who have embraced traditional policies to react with anything except opposition. Advocates of grading reform are better advised to be empathetic with these concerns and anticipate the following comments.

- "You're not preparing students for the real world!"
- "You'll never help low-performing kids if you don't increase rigor!"
- "What about high-performing students? Why should they suffer because we have to slow everything down for kids who are lazy and irresponsible?"
- "If I've learned anything in teaching, it's that if it doesn't count, students won't do it."
- "If students don't do the work, they deserve a zero, period."
- "Great—just what we need—another generation of coddled kids who can't take any criticism without dissolving into a puddle of tears."

This is a good start, but only the tip of the iceberg of complaints about proposed grading reform. We must be able to craft our responses so that the skeptics know that they are heard and respected. In fact, we can find common ground with the critics by embracing the need for rigor, discipline, and personal responsibility. The question is not whether we share these values, but rather how we can use the best available evidence to achieve those ends. This book makes clear that improved grading practices are more rigorous, encourage more personal responsibility, and have more dire consequences than toxic grading practices for students who are lazy and irresponsible. Here is an interesting conversation starter to use at the start of your next faculty meeting. Ask these two questions.

1. What causes student success?

2. What causes student failure?

It is very likely that faculty will list the terms *lazy* and *irresponsible* in response to the second question, along with factors such as inadequate parental support, poor personal organization, inadequate prior knowledge, inability to pay attention, and a litany of other purported causes. The purpose of posing those two questions is not to create an argument about whether or not they are true, but rather to consider, "If these causes are true, then what can we do to address them?" For example, if a cause of student failure is inadequate prior knowledge, then we should consider preassessments during the first week of every semester so that instruction and schedules can meet the needs of students. If the cause of student failure is that students are indeed lazy and irresponsible, then we should ask whether or not our previous responses—Fs and zeroes—have accomplished their aims. If our previous responses are effective, then we should be able to report record-low numbers of failures this year, because students will have learned from their past mistakes and left their laziness and irresponsibility at the classroom door. However, if failure rates remain persistently high, then we must acknowledge that prior solutions such as using grading as punishment have not been effective, and we must be willing to undertake some alternative solutions.

Mistake 3: The Minimum Fifty *or Credit Provided for* No Work

I know of no area of grading reform more controversial than the *minimum fifty*. The minimum fifty policy is born of a sound principle—that the intervals between grades should be equal. On a one hundred–point scale, where an A is equivalent to ninety points, a B equals eighty points, a C represents seventy points, and a D earns sixty points, but failing to complete work results in a zero, then the mathematics is simple. Advocates of that system are claiming that a failure is sixty points worse than wretched work that deserves sixty points. When combined with the use of the average to calculate final grades, the zero on a one hundred–point scale is the academic death penalty, with failures in the early days of the semester causing the successes of the later days of the semester to be meaningless. A few zeroes in the equation will cancel the effect of a dozen As. From this logic, many grading reform advocates have established policies that the lowest grade a teacher may give a student is fifty points—hence the minimum fifty. While this makes sense mathematically, it is a horrible way to communicate with teachers, parents, and community members. Giving students credit for no work contributes to the public perception that we are coddling students and giving them false impressions that they can do nothing and still get credit. Some critics say, "If I didn't show up for work, would I get 50 percent of my pay?" Both sides believe that their position is indisputably true. Rhetorical venom in a school board meeting, newspaper editorial, or faculty meeting is not the way to resolve this controversy. Participants in a community meeting hosted by a Midwestern school board on the subject of grading were disarmed when I said, "I agree with you! The minimum fifty is unfair and indefensible, so let's not do that. What we can do, however, is return to a traditional grading scale that we're all comfortable with—just like our traditional grade point averages. We report grades not on a one hundred–point scale, but rather on a time-honored, traditional scale in which A equals 4, B equals 3, C equals 2, D equals 1, and F equals 0. So, why not do that? This way, if a student doesn't hand work in, you can award a zero. Will that be acceptable to you?"

It makes the critics sound a bit silly when their central argument against giving students credit for missing work has been eliminated, and they still want to be angry after they have won the argument. At this point, I inevitably hear proponents of grading reform claim that a four–point scale is impossible because the computerized grading systems require a one hundred–point scale. That is nonsense. Every time I have heard this claim made, bar none, just a bit of inquiry reveals that it's not difficult at all to convert the computerized grading system to a range of zero to four rather than zero to one hundred. This reform is one of the most important things that schools can do to improve grading practices and reduce conflict with teachers, parents, and community members, yet otherwise thoughtful administrators persist in the claim that the one hundred–point scale is mandatory. This would be a good time to ask if technology vendors are the instructional leaders of the school system, or if that role should be left to the professional administrators and classroom educators in the schools.

Mistake 4: Dismissal of Homework

Participants in grading debates have fallen into two diametrically opposed camps, with some claiming that homework is essentially useless (Kohn, 2006) and others claiming that homework is vital (Zentall & Goldstein, 1999). One of the major complaints from teachers since the early days of the standards movement in the 1990s through the time of this printing is that they do not have enough time to address all required curriculum elements. The only possible means to cover required curriculum, they conclude, is to have students do work outside of class. In addition, advocates for work outside of class believe the successful completion of homework demonstrates personal responsibility, time management, and organization. Moreover, the practice that homework requires, they conclude, will lead to better student performance on exams and improved overall competency on academic standards. Critics of homework point to examples in which the tasks require hours of crushing boredom for students, assignments are unrelated to student proficiency, and the completion of homework assignments is more reflective of student compliance with teachers' demands than of demonstrated proficiency in meeting academic standards.

There is a reasoned middle ground between the advocates and critics of homework. It starts with acknowledging that practice is essential for learning any skill. The piano student who never practices outside of a lesson is unlikely to improve at the same pace as a student who practices diligently every day. Moreover, students who engage in independent practice can proceed at their own pace, with some slowing down for the most difficult challenges while others proceed at a faster pace. There is significant evidence that particular types of practice have a positive impact on student achievement. John Hattie (2009) refers to deliberative practice. Thus, both sides in the debate can agree that practice is essential but not just any sort of practice. The practice that most helps students is not merely a compliance drill to demonstrate what they already know, but rather the engagement in previously understood items and new and challenging problems. To see examples of this sort of practice in action, it is useful to watch a highly skilled music teacher or athletic coach. While some musical and athletic skills can be practiced at home, the most effective practice includes the focus on skills and problems of varying difficulty. While a music practice may begin with warm-ups that every student knows, the skillful music teacher then immediately moves not to the first measure of a piece of music, but rather to those parts of the music on which students need practice, feedback, and more practice. Effective athletic coaches do not send students home with a basketball in their backpacks with instructions to "do the odd-numbered problems, one through thirty," but rather engage students individually and in groups with the sort of practice that will most benefit their performance.

It is interesting to note that particularly effective practice occurs not at home in isolation, but at school, and is accompanied by feedback, repetition, and improvement. How can we acknowledge the need for practice and also accept the reality that in many cases, success in traditional homework assignments has much more to do with the home environment than the personal character and responsibility of students? As my principal told me years ago, the word *homework* may or may not have anything to do with the word *home*. Once we have defined the proper role of homework (practice for improved performance) and the best environment for homework (one that supports feedback, practice, and improved performance), we can validate the traditional demand for homework and also stop the stultifying and useless homework practices that so often prevail.

Mistake 5: Failure to Acknowledge the Limited Time of Teachers

Whatever academic standards your school is using, from the National Governors Association for Best Practices (NGA) and Council of Chief State School Officers' (CCSSO) Common Core State Standards (CCSS) to individual state standards and other provincial or national standards, I can make this prediction with certainty: there are too many standards and not enough time to cover all of them. Even standards documents that claim to be highly focused are undermined by the presumption that they address what a student should learn during a single academic year. While that sounds reasonable—and it is certainly more reasonable than previous versions of state standards that required more than three years to cover (Marzano, 2006)—even the versions of supposedly more focused standards are little consolation for the many teachers whose students are catching up academically. Such students require more than one year of learning to end the year at the grade-level proficiency required to enter the following year with confidence and success. Any administrator who attempts to cram more tasks into the teacher's day by dictating a longer list of tasks will face a high degree of frustration among both teachers and administrators.

If, for example, we expect teachers to have time to support the deliberative practice of students (as opposed to merely grading homework), provide timely feedback for students (as opposed to simply sending home report cards and flunk letters), and create a "Form B" of assessments so that students will persist until they are proficient, then we must creatively provide more time in the school day. Richard DuFour, Rebecca DuFour, Robert Eaker, and Thomas Many (2010) provide an excellent list of low- to no-cost methods for providing more time for teachers. Figure I.1 outlines several ways DuFour et al. (2010) suggest to adjust schedules to incorporate time for collaboration.

Common Preparation

Build the master schedule to provide daily common preparation periods for teachers of the same course or department.

Parallel Scheduling

Schedule common preparation time by assigning the specialists (physical education teachers, librarians, music teachers, art teachers, instructional technologists, guidance counselors, foreign language teachers, and so on) to provide lessons to students across an entire grade level at the same time each day.

Adjusted Start and End Time

Start the workday early, or extend the workday one day each week. In exchange for adding time to one end of the workday, teachers get the time back on the other end of that day. To make up for the twenty-five minutes the schedule shifted from instructional time to collaboration time, five minutes is trimmed from five of the eight fifty-minute class periods. By making these minor adjustments to the schedule one day each week, the entire faculty is guaranteed an hour of collaborative planning without extending their workday or workweek by a single minute.

Shared Classes

Combine students across two different grade levels or courses into one class for instruction. While one teacher or team instructs the students, the other team engages in collaborative work.

Group Activities, Events, and Testing

Teams of teachers coordinate activities that require supervision of students rather than instructional expertise, such as watching an instructional video, conducting resource lessons, reading aloud, attending assemblies, or testing. Nonteaching staff members supervise students while teachers engage in team collaboration.

Banked Time

Over a designated period of days, extend the instructional minutes beyond the required school day. After you have banked the desired number of minutes, end the instructional day early to allow for faculty collaboration and student enrichment. By teaching an extra ten minutes for nine days in a row, teachers "bank" ninety minutes. On the tenth day, instruction stops early in the afternoon, and the entire faculty has collaborative team time for two hours.

In-Service and Faculty Meeting Time

Schedule extended time for teams to work together on staff development days and during faculty meeting time. Rather than requiring staff to attend a traditional whole-staff in-service session or sit in a faculty meeting while directives and calendar items are read aloud, shift the focus and use of these days and meetings so members of teams have extended time to learn with and from each other.

Source: Adapted from DuFour et al., 2010, pp. 125–127.

Figure I.1: Making time for collaboration.

While the list in figure I.1 may not be exhaustive, it is certainly effective in reconciling the limitations of teacher time with the demands for improved collaboration, feedback, and support for student success.

When school leaders anticipate these five mistakes in advocating for grading reform, they can have a respectful and meaningful answer for almost every objection. While this will not mollify every opponent of improved grading practices, it will go a long way toward establishing a thoughtful dialogue. Opponents of improved grading practices almost always want the best for students, and they also want to have their concerns addressed with something other than an imperious command.

How to Get the Most Out of This Book

This book is meant to inspire teachers, administrators, school board members, and any other grading reform leaders to engage in conversation and take action collaboratively to improve and implement FAST grading policies that keep student learning at the forefront of education.

Part I guides grading reform leaders in building relationships with teachers, parents, and communities. Chapter 1 addresses common resistances to grading reform and poses considerations for gaining key stakeholder support. To help readers begin their own conversations about grading reform in their schools and districts and gain a deeper understanding of the culture and structure necessary to support change, chapters 2 and 3 ask readers to consider several scenarios of schools engaged in grading debates. While the scenarios are fictional, they are based on composites of real schools' and teachers' experiences.

Part II guides readers in the basics of implementing FAST grading and improving best practices. Chapter 4 provides a deep overview of the elements of FAST grading. Chapter 5 responds to the time crunch teachers often face by showing how FAST grading and time-saving strategies can improve efficiency of grading and feedback for students. Chapter 6 proposes best practices for addressing student behavior and how responses to behavior relate to grading and students' learning.

Part III invites readers to deepen their knowledge of FAST grading by examining the influence of best practices from colleagues in the school, system, and community. Chapter 7 considers how real-world lessons, drawn from the arts and physical education, can positively impact the ways educators implement and improve feedback and grading. Chapter 8 concludes with a fictional case study of a reorganized district to show readers how best practices for grading must also take into account the effect of a system's teaching and leadership practices.

This book is designed to be an interactive experience. At the end of each chapter, reflection sections ask readers to pause, ponder, and discuss the issues at hand. Although best suited for collaborative teams and colleagues to complete together, the exercises in these sections are easily adaptable for personal reflection and application as well. Please take a few moments while you are reading each chapter and, preferably with colleagues with whom you are studying the text, respond to the questions either in the pages of the book or in an electronic notepad. Additionally, a series of brief videos is available at Creative Leadership Solutions (http://creativeleadership.net), and they might be useful prompts for a faculty discussion of these topics.

Reflection

Which of the five mistakes discussed in the introduction have you observed or heard about? Use figure I.2 to frame, in your own words, how you might anticipate these mistakes in your school and avoid them.

Mistake	How to Avoid This Mistake
How Before *Why*	
Sympathy Over Rigor	
The *Minimum Fifty* or Credit Provided for No Work	
Dismissal of Homework	
Failure to Acknowledge the Limited Time of Teachers	

Figure I.2: Reflections on five common mistakes.

*Visit **go.solution-tree.com/assessment** for a free reproducible version of this figure.*

Part I

Building Relationships With Teachers, Parents, and Communities

Chapter 1

PREPARING FOR FAST GRADING

In a FAST grading system, policies are fair, accurate, specific, and timely. These policies support the most important purpose of grading—to provide feedback to students to improve their performance. Certainly, there are other purposes, such as reporting to parents and prospective colleges and even, in some schools, comparing students to one another. Whatever these secondary purposes might be, in a FAST grading school, it is essential to keep the primary purpose of grading in mind. Making changes to support a grading system that provides fair, accurate, specific, and timely feedback to students is not always an easy endeavor, however. This chapter explores changing the grading system (and with it, dealing with staff protests and common challenges to grading reform) and proposes considerations for gaining key stakeholder support. We'll also consider the next steps after deciding to change the grading system.

Changing the Grading System

Changes in grading systems are often the last things on the agenda for school reform, after many other instructional and leadership initiatives have been implemented. This is strange because changes in grading offer the opportunity for what Harvard professor John P. Kotter (1996) calls *short-term wins*, one of the key elements of effective change. For example, when the Cardinal Community School District in Iowa made a commitment to getting all homework finished on time every week by ensuring that the work was finished either at home or in school by Friday at noon, its failure rate dropped over 95 percent, suspensions were down 55 percent, and attendance improved (Reeves, 2012). This is not an unusual impact of grading reform as Thomas R. Guskey (2015) and Ken O'Connor (2011) attest. Schools that stop using the average to calculate the final grade and focus only on student performance against a standard at the end of the year will automatically have more students passing. In addition, fewer students whose efforts are futile will become hopeless troublemakers in the last two months of the semester. When final grades are based on averages, students who receive zeroes early in the semester often give up and stop learning when they realize that absolutely nothing they can do will help them pass the class, no matter how high their performance is at the end. Students, teachers, and administrators should be indignant when grading practices based on averages undermine their hard work.

Nevertheless, if educators try to change the grading system without adequate communication with parents and teachers, they will see a candlelight vigil held outside a board of education meeting with people demonstrating in favor of teachers' rights to use zeroes and averages. They will see state legislatures intervene to secure a teacher's right to use zeroes and averages. They will see parents come out in force to a board meeting protesting changes in grading systems that, mysteriously, the protesters also link to the Common Core State Standards. The two sides almost never meet except in confrontational circumstances. It is far more constructive to engage community members and parents informally through open and candid discussions. These are excellent ways to identify and debunk rumors and, instead, talk about the essential concerns that community members have heard. It is imperative that these meetings begin with the common goals that parents, community members, teachers, administrators, and students all share. This is an opportunity to reassure all stakeholders that you will continue to support a strong work ethic, have appropriate consequences for missing work, promote academic honors and recognition, and maintain individualized education programs (IEPs) for students with special needs.

This book does not guarantee that educators can win public relations battles against people who are not willing to engage in rational debate. But it does suggest some ways in which they can argue on behalf of the best interests of students, teachers, and school systems in a cogent way. Educators will never get 100 percent buy-in for any major change initiative, but they can get enough of a critical mass in order to make progress. Let's consider practical ways educators can increase buy-in and gain support for making changes to the grading system.

Preparing for the Firestorm

One of the best ways to avoid a firestorm of protest about grading is to ask some teachers to engage voluntarily in a pilot program. These teachers should be supported with professional learning opportunities and administrative support. The only requirement is that they show their results to their colleagues at the end of the pilot, specifically reporting changes in student performance, behavior, and grades. It's not necessary that teachers make many changes all at once, but rather they should select a change that they believe will have the greatest impact on the performance of their students. The following are three examples of pilot projects that teachers might select.

1. **Change the consequence for late or missing work:** Shift from *I don't accept late work* to *You must get the work done, even it means before school, during lunch, after school, or during a restricted study period—whatever it takes, you will get this work done*. Students, particularly in secondary schools, will soon find that peer pressure (such as the desire to have lunch with friends) will overcome reluctance to get work done.

2. **Change the grading scale from zero to one hundred to zero to four:** This is traditional and understandable— 4 equals A; 3 equals B; 2 equals C; 1 equals D; 0 equals F. It's exactly the way that grade point averages are typically calculated. It's not a new system, but a very traditional one that was in place for many decades before the advent of computerized systems that arbitrarily imposed the

zero– to one hundred–point scale. By rescaling the grading system to a span from zero to four points, teachers can still award a zero for missing work, but it is a mathematically accurate zero, with every grade level having one point of difference between them. When zeroes are awarded on a one hundred–point scale, with the C at seventy and the D at sixty but the failure to turn work in at zero, we are claiming that failing to turn work in is six times worse than turning in work that is truly wretched. Moreover, the zero in a one hundred–point scale becomes the academic death penalty, making it almost impossible for a student to recover.

3. **Stop using the average:** Make the final grade a matter of teacher professional judgment based on the student's performance against the standards. Some students "get it" early in the year, and others do not fully understand the material until the end of the year. Academic standards never say *learns algebra fast* or *masters historical concepts quickly*. Standards-based performance is founded on success as measured against the standard, and speed in learning is irrelevant.

These are just pilot projects for a few voluntary teachers who are willing to try something new. Before the firestorm over changes in grading policies begins, be prepared to have some very satisfied teachers, students, and parents speak out on behalf of successful pilot projects that have taken place in your own school system. Surely someone might object that this would mean that teachers will have different grading systems. As we have determined earlier, teachers already have different grading systems. Some will object that they cannot change the school's policy on the use of the average and zeroes. When I heard this statement from a group of secondary school faculty members, I suggested that we ask the principal who was standing nearby. So, somewhat timidly, the faculty asked if it was okay to try a pilot project on grading. "Of course!" the principal replied. "Please just keep me posted on how you're doing." Teachers have more power than they think, particularly when it comes to promising practices that will reduce failures, increase student engagement, and improve discipline. Armed with their experience in piloting these promising policies, teachers are poised to influence the critical mass of support needed to make substantive and lasting changes to grading practices. But what happens when other educators resist and defend toxic grading policies anyway? Let's consider how educators supporting change can respond effectively to naysayers.

Responding to Defenders of Toxic Grading Policies

There is not a teacher on earth who begins the day wondering, *What toxic teaching practices can I use today?* Teachers genuinely want to do the right thing for their students. It's important the advocates of changing grading practices (such as those in favor of using standards-based grading, grading on a four–point scale, and so on) acknowledge the goodwill and professionalism of teachers who are advocates of traditional practices. Let's consider common defenses of traditional practices that challenge grading reforms, and think about how advocates of grading reform might provide respectful responses.

- **Challenge 1:** "The reason I don't accept late work is that in the real world, you have to get your work done right the first time."

  Response: "This might have been true in the past, but the real world requires that people in the workforce submit work, get feedback, and then improve it. This cycle often repeats itself many times before work is finally submitted. We want to teach students not a one-and-done work ethic, but rather a work ethic that requires perseverance, the willingness to accept feedback, and then the understanding of how to use that feedback to improve their performance. That's the real world our students will enter in just a few years."

- **Challenge 2:** "The reason I award zeroes on the one hundred–point scale is simple: no work equals no points. Everybody understands that. Besides, not turning work in should be a severe penalty. Students need to know it's important to get work done."

Response: "I understand your position and how frustrating it must be for students to refuse, sometimes again and again, to turn in work. Your teaching surely can have a positive effect on them, perhaps getting them to change their behavior and start turning in their work. If you want to improve their behavior, then you might consider making your zeroes mathematically accurate by using the four, three, two, one, zero scale, representing A, B, C, D, and F, respectively. This is still the way that we calculate grade point averages, and it's the way that grades were calculated for many decades. This way, you can still award zeroes, but a student who learns from the value of diligence and work ethic can recover and still pass the class."

Challenge 3: "The reason I use the average is that I don't want students to slack off early in the semester and then think that they can make it up at the end. They need to come to school every day and work hard, from the first day of the semester through the last day. Besides, if it doesn't count as a grade, then students will never do the work."

Response: "I understand your desire for good student work ethic, and I'd like to ask you to reflect on your own classwork when you were a student, particularly in college or graduate school. Specifically, I'd like you to think about a class that was required but was quite unfamiliar to you. For many students in graduate school, this is the research and statistics class. For many students in undergraduate classes, it might be an assessment class. In any case, please think of a class in which, at the start, you were unfamiliar with the material—perhaps bewildered. The early weeks of the semester were immensely frustrating because you were being asked about things with which you had no familiarity. You not only didn't know about statistics and research but you saw little relevance between that class and your responsibilities. But it was a required course, so you persisted. About the middle of the course, you had one of those aha moments and everything started to make sense. From that point on, you aced the class and perhaps even enjoyed it a little bit. Every teacher and administrator I know has had this sort of experience in at least one college or graduate school class. The question is, Should you have been graded from the aha moment through the end of the class or on your average score from the beginning through the end of the class? It took a lot of diligence and work ethic to stick with this class rather than drop it, and that diligence and work ethic should have been rewarded. You probably expected the professor to reward you for your strong finish in the class, not the average of the beginning to the end of the class. At the very least, you wouldn't mind if the professor tried a pilot project in which students were evaluated based on their final performance and not the average."

- **Challenge 4:** "Standards-based grading is just grade inflation—more students getting higher grades for doing less work."

  Response: "This is partly true—more students do get higher grades in a standards-based grading system. But that's not because they do less work or that the teachers have lowered standards. Rather, it is because the teacher's response to missing or inadequate work is not a zero but the requirement that students redo the work, resubmit it, and respect teacher feedback. That's not grade inflation; that's work inflation. More work causes higher grades."

- **Challenge 5:** "Standards-based grading means the loss of honor rolls and academic honors."

  Response: "Many prestigious high schools and universities confer degrees with highest honors, high honors, and honors. This makes far more sense than the claim that the student who has a 3.998 grade point average is superior to the student with a 3.997 average."

These are not intended to be scripted responses. But they do provide a respectful tone to engage the opponents of grading reform. Before educators even try pilot projects, it might be useful to role-play the objections to grading reform and some of these respectful and thoughtful responses.

Gaining Key Stakeholder Support

While the primary purpose of grading is providing feedback to improve student performance and teaching practices, it is also important to note that grades have a wider audience. The governing boards, teachers and teachers' unions, parents and guardians, and students all have vested interests in grading policies for various reasons. To reform grading policies effectively, it is essential to address the concerns of each of these groups and gain their support for FAST grading.

Governing Boards

In educational systems, the governing board is a key stakeholder, and policy reform requires its clear and unequivocal support. The board should be encouraged to adopt a one-sentence grading policy: *The superintendent shall implement grading policies that are fair, accurate, specific, and timely and that advance the vision of the school system.* That's it—no percentages, no letter grades, no standards-based grading—nothing except this single sentence. This leaves room for the superintendent, teachers, and principals to differentiate where necessary and to conduct pilot projects. If an intervention or grading reform doesn't work, then the superintendent should be able to change it without going through a process of board approval. Having the governing board members vote on the details of a grading system makes as much sense as having them vote on the color of tile on the cafeteria floor. Neither is a policy issue.

Equipped with this one-sentence grading policy, the administrative leaders, teacher leaders, parents, and students can make the case to the board of how they are engaging in pilot projects and will, ultimately, craft school and district policies that meet the board's criteria.

Unfortunately, when grading becomes the subject of public controversy and the board has not been well informed before the controversy began, the board can find the arguments against grading reform very persuasive. In particular, boards of education have directed superintendents to repeal grading reforms such as the minimum fifty or second chances on tests and assignments because the board, understandably, wants to promote personal responsibility by students. This is why it is essential to give the board the research on the reforms that you are contemplating and also have pilot projects precede system-level implementation.

Additionally, it is important to show the benefit of grading reforms to the entire system. For example, advocates of grading reform might point to the improvement in students' personal responsibility because of accompanying provisions in grading reform that provide systems of clear consequences for students who miss assignments. One of the most immediate system-level impacts is a decreased failure rate— the source of enormous costs for repeated classes, summer school, and extra teaching staff. When a school of one thousand students reduces the failure rate from 40 percent to 20 percent, then the reduction of two hundred student failures accounts for more than the cost of a single full-time equivalent teacher. Because the failures likely involved different subjects, even more teaching staff are saved. In addition, the central office has a clear interest in reducing disciplinary problems, particularly suspensions and expulsions. Each of these requires a hearing and may also involve legal fees for the district. Finally, the district has an interest in improving the performance of every school in order to demonstrate the effectiveness of the entire system.

Teachers and Teachers' Unions

The teachers' union or association is another key stakeholder. Because the lack of time to get their jobs done professionally is a key concern of many teachers, it is vital to explain how grading reforms save time for every teacher. Most important, it reduces failure and improves discipline. Dealing with the parents of failing students, facing repeaters in class, and sitting in on suspension and expulsion hearings are all drains on teachers' time. Having students sandbag their work early in the semester and then try to get it all in at the end of the semester is another crushing burden on teachers' time. When grading reforms are presented to teachers, I suggest asking teachers to imagine a school year in which homework was completed every week, and regardless of whether or not it counted toward a final grade, students would engage in meaningful practice that led to better performance. I would ask them to imagine the beginning of a school year with no repeaters in their class. I would ask them to imagine the end of term with no students who were so defeated by the average and their accumulation of zeroes that they had nothing else to do but cause trouble. And I would ask them to imagine students at the end of the term who remain engaged because they know that every day they have the opportunity to do better, apply what they learned, and know that they are receiving credit for what they know, not how quickly they learned it.

Finally, with less time and fewer staff allocated for students repeating a grade or a class, consider how many more electives could be added to the schedule to engage every teacher's creative and intellectual abilities. When a substantial number of students are repeating classes, teachers who would prefer to teach electives and advanced courses to highly motivated students wind up teaching basic classes to unmotivated students. It's a simple formula: fewer failures allow for more electives and advanced courses. This is also helpful to art, music, and other nonrequired courses, because students who fail almost always lose some of the most motivating courses of their school day. Grading reform, therefore, has the potential to help every teacher in the school.

Parents and Guardians

Parents and other caregivers are particularly interested in student grades, and they often find them baffling. The move to standards-based grading has introduced terminology with which many parents are unfamiliar, particularly if their own experience in school consisted solely of letter grades. In addition, many parents find the phrase *meets standards* confusing, as some teachers use that term to consider student performance against a standard at the end of the year, while other teachers estimate what students should be learning throughout the year. In the latter case, a student who is clearly not meeting grade-level standards will nevertheless receive a mark of meeting standards based on the teacher's estimate of where the student should be at that particular point in time. The ambiguity and inconsistency of these marks leads some parents to distrust and oppose the entire standards-based grading movement. Guskey (2003) poses the question in his book *How's My Kid Doing? A Parent's Guide to Grades, Marks, and Report Cards.* Just as students need FAST grading that is fair, accurate, specific, and timely, so parents also need that sort of feedback on their children's performance.

Parent stakeholders are essential, particularly in an age in which Twitter chats, Google Hangouts, and other public forums provide an echo chamber in which people around the world with similar beliefs will reinforce every point of opposition to grading reform, both those that are legitimate and those that are based on fantastic rumors. To be fair, the same echo chamber–effect happens in the chat rooms frequented by advocates of grading reform, with rarely a single critical voice to challenge prevailing wisdom. Parents deserve a respectful hearing and thoughtful response. Parents of academically advanced students are particularly vocal in grading debates, at least in part because traditional grading systems serve as a means to allow academically advanced and well-organized students to be clearly distinguished from their classmates. Consider valedictorian awards, in which the difference between the first and second place in a class can be a few one-hundredths of a point. Perhaps this is because a student took band in ninth grade and didn't receive a quality point (that is, an extra point in the grade point average sometimes awarded for advanced classes) for the class. This can be very threatening to parents who have invested their hopes in a child who aspires to be valedictorian.

Parents also want to be certain that their children are prepared for the challenging work ahead in college and the world of work. Therefore, some of the generalizations made about college grading systems must be challenged. For example, at the Massachusetts Institute of Technology (MIT) and Wellesley College, two top-notch institutions, first-year students do not receive grades, but instead receive feedback on their performance. Why? Because the administrators recognize that students in these schools have rarely experienced any grade south of an A, and they have not experienced much in the way of negative feedback. By eliminating grades for first-year students but preserving honest feedback, MIT and Wellesley prepare students for the rigorous years ahead and allow professors to give honest feedback without fear of complaints from students, parents, and—stunningly—lawyers prepared to challenge grades that a student regards as inappropriate. In brief, traditional grading systems are not what make a college experience rigorous. Rather, rigor is the result of an academic environment in which students receive and respond to feedback that will best prepare them for college and the world of work.

Students

Student stakeholders are absolutely essential in making the case for improved grading practices. In fact, of the 150 variables influencing student achievement (Hattie, 2012), the greatest impact was the ability of students to predict their final grade with accuracy. This ability is not the result of a student having extrasensory perception, but rather the result of continuous feedback throughout the marking period that allows students to know precisely where they stand and how to improve their final grade.

To an extent, clear feedback relies on clear expectations established at the beginning of the course or school year. One way many teachers establish clear expectations for assignments is through the use of scoring rubrics that outline specific criteria to demonstrate mastery. To check students' understanding of the expectations, ask students to underline or highlight the features of the expectations that they see in their own work. If a scoring rubric for an essay, lab report, or mathematics problem is sufficiently specific, it is not necessary for the teacher to write comments on student work. All that is necessary is to highlight or underline the phrases from the scoring rubric that best describe the student's work. Schools can use this protocol with performance rubrics, behavioral expectations, and anything else that we expect students to do.

Including students in the grading process requires six elements.

1. Clear expectations of performance expressed in student-accessible language

2. Student review and evaluation of anonymous work

3. Revision of evaluations based on collaboration with teacher and fellow students

4. Student self-evaluation

5. Revision of self-evaluation based on collaboration with teacher and fellow students

6. Student evaluation of work independently before it is turned in; then student comparison of the predicted grade to the grade received

If grading practices include these six elements early in the school year, then students should be able to predict their grades accurately by the first grading period. In addition, students should be able to communicate clearly with their parents about their grades and how those grades were earned. This replaces the typical conversation between students and parents about report cards.

> **Parent:** How'd you get that grade?
>
> **Student:** I dunno. I guess the teacher didn't like me.

With these six elements, there is no longer a reason for grading mystery, nor is grading the exclusive province of unknown teacher judgments. They certainly do not suggest that "the customer is always right." Students are certainly not customers who seek instant gratification. Rather, these six elements mean that student expectations and teacher expectations are closely aligned. Most important, when there is a difference between student and teacher assessment of work, the student can narrow those differences by close collaboration with the teacher and fellow students.

The challenge is that many of the most vocal, articulate, and influential students have been served very well by traditional grading practices. They are vying for academic honors that are competitive in nature—there is, after all, only one valedictorian at many schools. Grading systems that allow them to succeed and cause others to fail are clearly in their best interests. This is magnified in states where the top 10 percent automatically receive scholarships or acceptance into prestigious state schools. These promote a winner-takes-all competition among students in which the adage attributed to Gore Vidal is the ruling code of conduct: "It is not enough that I succeed. Others must fail" (Quote Investigator, 2012). A FAST grading system allows for students to distinguish themselves, but they must do so against a set of rigorous standards, not by merely beating a classmate.

Taking the Next Steps

Grading reform is one of the most controversial issues in education. The sides in the debate can be contentious, even rancorous, challenging one another's motives and concern for students. No matter how significant the research, critics of grading reform want to know if changes in grading will really influence their students in a positive way. Let's step back from the brink and attempt a more rational dialogue with the critics of standards-based grading, the four–point grading scale, the minimum fifty mandates, the elimination of averages, and late-work submission policies. There are several areas of common ground that every participant in the grading debate can find. All parties can, for example, agree on the value of rigor, work ethic, accuracy, and fairness.

I've been to enough parent meetings on this subject to know that mutual respect and understanding work far better than expert pronouncements. Both sides in this debate love students and want the best for them. With courtesy and common aims well established, it is possible to seek common ground on grading. But if reform is seen only as a means to go easy on students who are late in completing homework or other assignments, it is a nonstarter with the vast majority of teachers and administrators. Therefore, it is essential to begin the discussion not with grading reform, but rather with what academic and behavioral performance educators want from students. To establish these aims, most teachers and parents might come up with a list that looks something like this.

- Students should meet academic standards.

- Students should be respectful and kind.

- Students should be responsible and well organized.

- Students should perform well on tests and assignments.

What other expectations would unite almost all teachers and administrators in your school?

After identifying these common expectations, the next step in a fruitful discussion is about the degree to which your school achieves those expectations. In most schools, these expectations are not met, and in fact, student performance in these areas is declining. For the expectations that you identified, please identify the degree to which your school meets or does not meet them in figure 1.1.

Expectations	Met or Not Met	Reasons

Figure 1.1: Identifying and meeting expectations.

*Visit **go.solution-tree.com/assessment** for a free reproducible version of this figure.*

As a result of the exercise in figure 1.1, it should be clear that most present policies for grading are not meeting their purposes. Grades, when used as punishments and rewards, simply do not work (Guskey, 2015), and the data from your own school should make that clear. Then, it is appropriate to consider the ideas in this book to at least try, on a pilot basis, some alternative grading policies that have been shown to improve student performance and reduce discipline problems.

Here are some suggestions for next steps in implementing grading reform and reporting the results to colleagues in a school and educational system.

First, consider the data from the previous term. Just focus on the D and F grades, and ask, "What is the reason this student received a D or an F?" It's possible that the responses will include poor attendance and failures on final examinations. But it is also likely that the most common reason for low grades is the failure to turn in homework and other assignments. Before you try any grading policy changes, you can address the question in your own school, "Are our present grading policies effective?" If a significant number of student failures are the result of missing homework and other assignments, then it is fair to reconsider those grading policies. This is particularly true when the students in question are proficient on external tests, such as state assessments, but receive low grades in classes.

Second, consider very specific action research projects that address a specific grading innovation and the impact on student performance. For example, a teacher might volunteer to try eliminating the zero on a one hundred–point scale and replacing it with a four, three, two, one, zero scale. Another teacher might volunteer to try changing the weight of homework to 5 percent and weighting summative assessments more heavily. Another teacher volunteer might try eliminating the use of the average and focusing on final student performance. Each of these teachers would then present a simple two-bar graph. The first bar would show student failures last year, and the second bar would show student failures this year, after the reform in grading took place. Teachers might also add their qualitative observations about student engagement, teacher morale, student discipline, and so on.

Third, reconfigure the schedule so that teachers have time to collaboratively score student work. It's important to track two critical variables each time this scoring conference takes place: (1) the degree of agreement among teachers and (2) the time required to complete the scoring. The degree of agreement is a simple calculation— the plurality score divided by the total number of teachers. For example, if there are ten teachers in the group, and six of them score the student work with a 3, then the degree of agreement is 60 percent (six divided by ten). The introduction provided a number of ideas for reconfiguring the schedule, but collaborative scoring does not depend on a major configuration. Principals could give up the next faculty meeting, make all announcements in writing, and devote that time to collaborative scoring within a grade level or department.

It is essential for school leaders to recognize that massive change imposed from higher headquarters almost never works. It is much better to have local advocates for changes who can say to their colleagues with complete authenticity, "I know that we had doubts about this, but I've tried it, and it really works with our kids. Failure rates are down, discipline is better, students are more engaged, and I'm feeling better about my career."

FAST grading is not a miracle cure. But it can have a faster and more effective impact on student achievement and discipline than any other reform. People can see results within a single semester, giving local evidence of effectiveness. Teacher morale can improve within a single year because of reduced failure rates. System costs can be lowered within a single year because of fewer students in summer school and fewer students repeating classes.

Reflection

If you want to make an impact for students, teachers, schools, and systems, FAST grading is the right place to start. With your team, respond to the following.

1. Please identify one or more pilot projects that you plan to try over the next grading period. This doesn't have to include every faculty member; include only those who are willing to express a hypothesis about grading and then test that hypothesis with their own students. Consider the following ideas.

   ◊ Change the consequence for late or missing work.

   ◊ Change the grading scale to zero to four.

   ◊ Stop using the average.

2. How will you gain key stakeholder support? Consider the following stakeholders.

   ◇ Governing boards

   ◇ Teachers and teachers' unions

   ◇ Parents and guardians

   ◇ Students

3. What could be the next step in grading reform for your school? Choose just one idea that you believe would engage a significant number of teachers on a voluntary basis.

4. Conduct a quick poll of your students and ask them to predict their grade. In the left-hand column of figure 1.2, enter the students' names, in the middle column enter the students' self-predicted grades, and in the right-hand column enter your assessment of the students' work. What do you notice about the similarities and differences between student assessment and teacher assessment?

Student Name	Student Self-Assessment	Teacher Assessment

Figure 1.2: Exploring alignment between student self-assessment and teacher assessment.

*Visit **go.solution-tree.com/assessment** for a free reproducible version of this figure.*

5. What are some strategies you could implement immediately in order to close the gap between students' assessment of their performance and the teacher's assessment?

As we look ahead to chapter 2, keep your responses to the reflection questions in mind. In chapter 2, we'll observe schools in one district struggle to find common ground in defining fair grading policies and clear expectations for student learning.

Chapter 2

FINDING COMMON GROUND IN THE GRADING DEBATE

Too much of the time devoted to grading policy is where the devil is—in the details. How shall we grade homework? What is the weight of the final exam? What is the role of extra credit? To what extent can teachers override the policy with their professional judgment? One method to resolve these controversies is with policies of Byzantine complexity. Teachers can explain their grading rationale with mathematical precision, certain to overcome any challenge from a student or parent. Boards of education leap into the fray, attempting to bring some order to the chaos of idiosyncratic grading systems by imposing a board policy that provides the illusion of consistency. But the result of overly standardized policies, whether initiated in the classroom or the boardroom, is that the fundamental principles of grading are lost in the battle over policy details.

In this chapter, we consider the experiences of three fictional schools in the same school district, Patterson Elementary School, Singh Middle School, and North High School. Each of these schools tackles challenges with grading, from communicating to parents, and creating a schoolwide grading policy to establishing a grading system that helps prepare students for the rigors of high school and beyond. After you read about each school, consider the discussion questions and action steps with colleagues in your school. How would your school's faculty and administration respond in situations similar to those Patterson Elementary School, Singh Middle School, and North High School experienced? Additional educators' experiences with grading reform, leadership, and changing school culture can be found in chapter 8 for further study and reflection.

Patterson Elementary School

Barbara Fitch was having a bad day. She was the mother of two teenagers, an experienced fourth-grade teacher, and a marathoner who felt as fit and active as she appeared in her college graduation picture almost twenty years previously. Born to a two-teacher home, she started her career immediately after graduating from college and, after two decades in the profession, found herself the most experienced teacher at Patterson Elementary School. Until the retirement of three veteran staffers last year, Ms. Fitch always considered herself part of the younger crowd, and now here she was, the unofficial curmudgeon of the faculty. "When did I become the old one?" she wondered. What made this day particularly bad was how an ordinary faculty meeting had ended with tension, hurt feelings, and implications of unprofessionalism. Although Ms. Fitch had always been the peacemaker on the staff, helping to resolve conflicts and guide the faculty through six principals in the past twenty years, this meeting was not one in which she could forsake her values in the pursuit of peace.

The issue was grading and, in particular, how a parent, Sandra Jackson, had used the public comment portion of the school board meeting to attack—at least that's how it felt to Ms. Fitch—the teachers at Patterson. The meeting aired on the local cable television station's public access channel, and Ms. Jackson used her two minutes to her advantage.

Ms. Jackson had three children at Patterson in the third, fourth, and fifth grades. Although she held down a full-time job as a home health aide and her husband worked long hours in construction, she made a point of checking her children's homework and backpacks. She made healthy lunches for her kids, limited their screen time at home, and thought she was doing everything right.

Then came the first-term report cards. Sheila, the third grader, received straight As; Robert, the fourth grader in Ms. Fitch's class, received three Ps, an S, and an IP (Proficient, Satisfactory, and In Progress, respectively). Louisa, the fifth grader, received two Cs, a D, and two Fs. Louisa's teacher also suggested that Ms. Jackson meet with her immediately.

"How can this be?" Ms. Jackson demanded at the meeting. She continued. "All of my kids do good work. They may not be star students, but I watch them every night and send them to school ready to learn. I teach them to respect their teachers and don't take any excuses. But I don't know what to say to them when they all sit around the same kitchen table doing what I ask them to do. How can it be that one is an honor student and another is failing? The other has grades I don't even understand. It just doesn't make any sense to me."

During the faculty meeting, Aletha Simpson, the principal, never got her agenda off the ground.

"Who *is* this woman?" asked Jess Stein, a second-grade teacher.

"She's actually very nice and incredibly responsible," replied Sheila's third-grade teacher, Morgan Pearson. "I've had both of her older kids, and they were always fine with me."

"Sandra Jackson certainly never gave me any trouble," added one of the team members from Louisa's fifth-grade class. "We just needed to get her attention, and I guess we did that. Once the parents see that their kids aren't as perfect as they thought, maybe they will ensure that the homework gets done on time."

Ms. Fitch was unusually silent, stinging from the criticism of her new grading policy. She was part of a pilot project for proficiency-based grading, but it was clear from Ms. Jackson's complaint that the P, S, and IP grades were not helping parents understand what their children needed. After all, Ms. Jackson was one of the most conscientious parents Ms. Fitch had encountered, and if she was mad enough to go to the school board with her complaints, what must other parents think?

"I'll give her a call," said the principal. "I'm sure we can straighten this out."

"I'm not so sure about that," said Ms. Fitch quietly. "For all of the time we have spent collaborating with one another about curriculum, standards, discipline policies, and everything else, it looks like we have some pretty serious disagreements about grading. We're all professionals, and we should be able to get these issues on the table and resolve them."

"There's nothing to resolve," said James Winston, a fourth-grade teacher who rarely spoke in a faculty meeting. "You have your grading policies," he said to Ms. Fitch, "and I have mine. The last thing we need around here is another schoolwide mandate. Ms. Jackson can be as angry as she wants, but I don't think any of us should cave in because of an angry comment on cable television. If we do that, it just promotes bad behavior."

Ms. Fitch was stunned. While she and Mr. Winston had been on the same team, they had never discussed grading or much of anything else that was substantive. She had no idea that he was as upset as he seemed. Worse yet, she didn't realize how closed Mr. Winston was to having a professional conversation to resolve controversies. As the chime signaled the end of the hour, the faculty rose silently and left the room.

When teachers establish their own separate grading policies with different scales and different criteria, parents and students are often confused about what the grades really mean. But as the conflict between Ms. Fitch and Mr. Winston illustrates, it is not always easy to gain the support necessary to shift to a schoolwide standards-based grading system. In the next example, we'll see how a middle school's articulation of its vague goals contribute to a growing sense of resistance and division between teachers and the principal.

Singh Middle School

"We've got to get them ready for high school," Principal Ellen Singh said. The principal, who was no relation to Singh Middle School's namesake, could not have been more emphatic. She had just received the data on the performance of last year's eighth-grade students, 40 percent of whom had failed at least one course their freshman year of high school. While every teacher in Singh heard and understood the urgency in the principal's voice, no one understood what she meant. Were they to be tough, as the high school teachers claimed to be? Were they to do a better job of imparting learning? Were they to share skills, such as note-taking and asking for assistance? Were they to fail their eighth graders at unprecedented levels so that only the best-prepared students ever made it to ninth grade? Every hypothesis had an advocate, although evidence accompanied few, if any, hypotheses.

Ms. Cydell Jefferson, a veteran social studies teacher, spoke first. "Bad high school practice has never justified bad middle school practice," she said. "They think they are tough," she continued, referring to the high school faculty, "but if that strategy really worked, then why are there twelve hundred students in the ninth-grade class and six hundred students in the senior class?"

It was a statistic that was such a permanent fixture of North High School that few people thought to question it. But the truth was that Lincoln, the oldest high school in the district, was the *dragnet magnet*, as many knew it. If students didn't succeed at North, then they transferred to Lincoln. This phenomenon kept the dropout statistics low, while masking the dramatic failure rate of students who began their high school careers at North. Equipped with four tracks per grade, Lincoln had a clear protocol. If students had trouble in Advanced Placement (AP) classes, they were dropped to honors classes with significantly less homework and fewer demands. If they had trouble in honors, then they dropped to academic classes, which required nothing except attendance. And if they had trouble in academic classes, then they dropped to general education classes, where everyone received an A unless, the unfunny faculty joke went, he or she was convicted of felonious assault. A significant number of academic and general education students completed high school, many earning academic honors based on their grade point averages. Lincoln was known as the place that saved high school students who could not succeed in any other environment.

Back in the Singh faculty meeting, Ms. Jefferson's comments were met with stony silence. The school, having been recently reconstituted for poor performance, followed state law for low-performing schools, and had a new principal and new faculty members—more than 50 percent of the staff. The climate of fear was palpable. Principal Singh avoided the glare of Ms. Jefferson and asked if there were any more questions in a tone that clearly conveyed that more questions were not welcome.

Later that afternoon, a few of the new teachers who had been, very reluctantly, assigned to Singh came into Ms. Jefferson's room. They were surprised to see a number of students who were patiently waiting for Ms. Jefferson's support. While the contract day ended at 2:45 p.m., it was after 4:00 p.m. and Ms. Jefferson remained as patient as ever, giving each student one-to-one attention. When the last student left at about 4:30 p.m., the teachers approached her.

"You were very brave to speak up in the faculty meeting," said Mr. Leland Staniford.

"I can't believe that you stood up to the principal," said Ms. Michaela Sullivan.

"I don't get it," said Ms. Louisa Capuano. "You acted like a burned-out teacher, but here you are treating your students like gold—like a first-year teacher. What's up?"

Ms. Jefferson shifted in her chair uncomfortably. "I'm no hero," she began. "I just need to speak the truth. And I'm not that old—it's just my twenty-fifth year of teaching, and I started at twenty-one, so please don't make me sound like Methuselah. I've seen more than a dozen principals come and go, and in my next twenty years of teaching, I'll probably see another dozen. I respect Principal Singh and I wish her well, but I just don't see much value in threatening teachers with the whole 'we've got to get them ready for high school' speech. I've seen that many times."

"But what are we supposed to do?" asked Mr. Staniford.

"You're not supposed to do anything," replied Ms. Jefferson. "Just do what you think is right. I don't think it's right to treat middle school students like factory workers, and I don't think it's right to bully them into becoming North's perfect kids or Lincoln's rejects. I just want to love them because, at this age, I may be the only person who does. I'm not a pushover—watch them come in after school and ask for extra help. They do that because they know that I expect more out of them than what they do in class. But they also know that even if they try and fail, I will love and accept them anyway. And it's quite right that this probably doesn't prepare them for high school and college, where few adults love and accept them, but I do it anyway."

Her colleagues were stunned, not knowing what to ask next. "I wish I could offer you better advice," concluded Ms. Jefferson, "but that's all I've got."

As the teachers left her room, they saw Principal Singh's car leave the parking lot, probably headed to a meeting at the central office, followed by a board meeting that typically lasted until midnight. None of them doubted Principal Singh's commitment and competence, but they worried about the disconnect between the principal's dedication and Ms. Jefferson's experience and personal commitment to individual students.

When schools and systems do not clearly articulate their expectations for student learning, however well-intentioned they may be, the potential for misunderstanding grows. Even if faculty commit wholeheartedly to expectations like Principal Singh does, a lack of schoolwide, specific, evidence-based goals to achieve those expectations contributes to staff division and poor outcomes for students. In the next section, we'll see how blind commitment to the promise of student success without commonly understood goals affects students and teachers.

North High School

"You can't argue with success!" That was the ebullient response that Sanford Smythe had to nearly every concern he had heard during his ten years as the principal of North High School. Although the student population had changed, with increasing numbers of immigrant families whose children were learning English and a striking increase in the number of students eligible for free lunch, the test results were undeniably good. In fact, they were a close second to the magnet high school that students from affluent families largely populated.

"All of our students are gifted," Principal Smythe liked to say with an edge to his voice. "And we don't need anyone from the central office to label them that way."

He could afford to take a tough stance, as his retirement after thirty years of service was only a few months away.

Known as a strong leader who tolerated little in the way of dissent, the refrain of "You can't argue with success!" was used to settle controversies among parents, students, coaches, and especially the faculty. The way that things worked, particularly when it came to academic recognition, had changed little from Principal Smythe's days as a student at North. Based on the grade point averages from grades 9 through 12, there was a valedictorian, a salutatorian, and then the honors graduates—the top 10 percent of the twelfth-grade graduating class. The pictures outside of his office were testimonies to Principal Smythe's view of academic excellence, with the pictures of the school's ten most recent valedictorians on the right and the ten salutatorians on the left.

"Everybody doesn't get a trophy," he was fond of saying, "and everybody isn't a winner. Our job in high school is to get these kids ready for the challenging world of college and work, and that is precisely what we are doing."

What Principal Smythe never saw, however, was the way in which teachers mocked his confidence in success behind his back and the way in which some parents gamed the system to ensure that their children made it to the top 10 percent.

"Can't argue with success?" scowled Mr. Howard Leland, a mathematics teacher. "It's easy to be successful when at the first sign of trouble the counselors get the kids to transfer to another school or down to a lower track. The only reason we don't have any big problems here is that we export them to our friends at Lincoln," referring to the district's other high school that was not the magnet school for the gifted.

Lincoln was widely recognized for being a warm, nurturing, and welcoming place for high school students—particularly for those who had encountered difficulty elsewhere. Lincoln boasted a distinguished list of alumni, although it was consistently ranked last among the three high schools in test performance. Some of the preliminary analyses of scores based on academic growth suggested that Lincoln succeeded in building relationships with many students who had been unsuccessful elsewhere. Many of Lincoln's students arrived in ninth grade as struggling readers. Rather than immediately labelling students as failures like their counterparts at North did, the Lincoln faculty gave students an opportunity to succeed. But this was a mixed blessing. Some students used this environment as an opportunity for personal and academic resilience—and they were the Lincoln success stories. Other students, however, used the relaxed environment simply to continue the habits that had led them to suffer academically in the first place. Therefore, the same nurturing, loving, and accepting environment worked to restore some students to academic success and doomed other students to the illusion of success—good grades without good performance. While Lincoln had a stage full of students receiving academic honors, the graduation ceremonies at North were quite different, where the best students were separated from the rest with mathematical precision.

For most of the past decade, parents had supported Principal Smythe's version of academic Darwinism, as North consistently sent a few of its six hundred students to elite universities and more than half of the graduates attended some sort of college or technical school. The rest found jobs, stayed with their parents, or joined the military. The least successful transferred to Lincoln where, the entire community knew, it was easy to earn a diploma. It was only in the past couple of years that some parents and faculty members began to challenge the accuracy and fairness of the academic recognition system at North. Dr. Frank Martinez and Mrs. Consuelo Martinez had sent all four of their children to

North, each one going on to college. A well-respected community college professor, Dr. Martinez took enormous satisfaction in
the success of his children, even as he saw his youngest struggle to
achieve the academic honors that her older siblings had enjoyed.
Sonia had worked as hard—even harder—than her older siblings and
achieved similar grades. But rather than being in the top 10 percent,
she found herself in the middle of the class rank, far behind her
peers who were marked as academically competitive.

Without her knowledge, Sonia was the subject of a heated discussion among teachers. "She's one of the best students I have ever had,"
said Mr. Joe Cleland, the mathematics teacher. "She always takes on
challenges, including the toughest classes, and perseveres even when
she has difficulty at first. She works harder for a B-minus than most
students in this school work for an A."

"Absolutely," said Ms. Luanne Mozingo, the chair of the English
language arts department. "Sonia writes essays on Shakespeare and
W. E. B. Du Bois, supports her fellow students in class, and meets
almost every deadline. Besides, a B in my class is worth an A in every
other class in the department."

"So what's the problem?" asked Dr. Andrew Yates, a new
counselor at the school. "She sounds like a great student. Who's
complaining?"

"Her parents," said Mr. Cleland and Ms. Mozingo almost in
unison. Mr. Cleland continued, "Frank Martinez is a great parent and
teacher. He didn't need to get a doctorate to teach in the community college, but he did it in his forties while he was putting three
kids through college. Mrs. Martinez is one of our most enthusiastic
volunteers, and she's the director of the athletic center many of our
students use. But they are irate that Sonia is not receiving academic
honors this year."

"If Sonia is that great, why are her grades so mediocre?" asked
Dr. Yates.

"They wouldn't have been mediocre five years ago," replied
Ms. Mozingo, "but they are today because every time students at this
school get into academic difficulty, we put them in a less-challenging

class where they can get an A if they avoid a violent offense for the semester."

"That's an exaggeration," added Mr. Cleland. "But not much of one. We have students who are receiving high grades in mathematics classes when they are not doing work any more challenging than they had in middle school."

"And our creative writing classes?" said Ms. Mozingo. "That's where students who are reading and writing on a seventh-grade level go to get affirmation after they are transferred out of grade-level courses. They learn enough to be called *proficient* on the state tests, but the cutoff score is so ridiculously low that we have validated test prep more than learning. They make the school look good, but we are cheating them out of their future."

"So what do you propose to do about it?" asked Dr. Yates. "Surely Principal Smythe knows that this is a problem."

"Great—you tell him," said Mr. Cleland. "But I'll save you the time because I already know the answer: you can't argue with success! Besides, Frank and Consuelo Martinez are not the only parents with children in the school. The ones who have the attention of the administration are very happy with the academic honors policy because they know how to game the system. Whenever their kids have less than a stellar grade in class, they drop the class or take summer school. We even have kids transferring in online course credits from high schools where their parents can buy a high grade that goes onto our transcripts. It's working great for the top 10 percent, as long as you mean the top 10 percent of income, not the top 10 percent of academic performance."

"All right, I believe you," replied Dr. Yates. "The immediate problem is, what do we do about Sonia? In my last school, I saw really talented kids get frustrated, crash, and burn when they thought the system wasn't fair. It sounds as if she deserves better treatment than she has received in the past three years."

"Don't expect her to ask for help," said Ms. Mozingo. "Her parents may complain, but Sonia would be mortified if she thought that she was getting any special treatment. She's desperately trying to live up to the reputations of her siblings. She occasionally lets her fears slip through in her writing, and frankly I'm worried about her."

"I've got papers to grade," said Mr. Cleland, as he left the room.

"I've got four discipline problems waiting in my office," said Dr. Yates.

"I think I need to speak with Sonia's parents," said Ms. Mozingo.

As the conversation between Sonia's teachers and her guidance counselor illustrate, inconsistent grading policies and curricular expectations contribute to an unfair system where persistence goes unacknowledged and letter grades, rather than student learning, become the measure of success. From the district level to the classroom level, discrepancies in grading policies and expectations leave teachers, students, and parents guessing about the real meaning and extent of students' academic proficiency.

Reflection

To address, correct, and prevent challenges with grading like those that Patterson Elementary School, Singh Middle School, and North High School experience, think back on your own experiences in difficult conversations about grading with faculty, administrators, students, and parents. With your colleagues, first reflect on the case studies this chapter presents in questions 1 through 5. Then, use questions 6 through 8 to guide your action steps for establishing FAST grading practices in your classroom, school, or district.

1. Think about the people in each case study.

    a. **At Patterson Elementary:** Ms. Fitch, the fourth-grade teacher who is piloting a standards-based grading policy; Mr. Winston, who prefers to maintain his own policy and appears unwilling to discuss the issue; and Ms. Pearson, the third-grade teacher for Sheila

    b. **At Singh Middle School:** Ms. Jefferson, the veteran social studies teacher; her fellow teachers, Ms. Sullivan, Ms. Capuano, and Mr. Staniford; and Principal Singh

    c. **At North High School:** Mr. Cleland, the mathematics teacher; Ms. Mozingo, the English language arts chair; Dr. Yates, the counselor; and Principal Smythe

With whom do you identify the most? What about him or her resonates with you? What questions would you ask the other teachers and the principal at the respective schools?

2. Can you find any common ground among the people in each case study? Without minimizing their important differences of opinion, what are the principles that they might hold in common?

3. Think of times when you have observed disagreements among educators and administrators. What were the most effective ways in which these disagreements were resolved? What strategies were least effective?

4. Consider the viewpoints of the principals, Aletha Simpson, Ellen Singh, and Sanford Smythe. What role should they play in the discussions with the teachers and parents at Patterson Elementary School, Singh Middle School, and North High School, respectively?

5. Put yourself in the role of parents.

    a. Ms. Jackson, the parent of the Patterson Elementary School students, Louisa, Robert, and Sheila

    b. A parent of a Singh Middle School student

    c. Frank and Consuelo Martinez, and their youngest child, Sonia, a student at North High School

What are their most important needs? What are their responsibilities to help to resolve these issues? What challenges would you place before the administration and faculty?

6. Working with your colleagues, develop of list of principles that might guide your future grading policies. Remember

that principles are not policies, but common values on which you can all agree. For example, you might decide that truth is a universal principle. People can disagree about how to arrive at truth in grading, but most people will agree that it's a good principle to guide future decisions. What are your common principles?

7. Identify at least one policy that you experienced as a student, from kindergarten through graduate school, that violated one of the group's principles. For example, if one of your fundamental principles is fairness, when were you treated unfairly as a result of a teacher's or professor's grading policies?

8. What grading policies are in use in your classroom and school that best exemplify the principles you have identified? What are your personal experiences with the best practices in grading?

At every level of the school, educators have responsibilities to students, to parents and guardians, and to their fellow colleagues to create and uphold grading policies that support student learning. In systems that have inconsistent, poorly articulated learning expectations from the classroom level to schoolwide level, students' learning, teachers' effectiveness, and administrators' leadership suffer as a result. In chapter 3, we'll look at how three teachers dealt with these issues by getting tough, getting even, and getting real about grading policies in their schools.

GAINING TEACHERS' PERSPECTIVES ON GRADING

The teachers and administrators profiled in chapter 2 were not malicious. They had every good intention in the world. They have seen the consequences when teachers and professors attempt to be popular rather than effective, perhaps in their own lives and in the academic experiences of their students. They also shared a bone-deep belief that when they expected more out of their students, they usually got better results. Many of them received students from other schools or from previous grade levels in their own schools who lacked the organizational skills, disciplinary knowledge, and academic fundamentals necessary to succeed. In this chapter, we will consider three grading scenarios from teachers' points of view. Although the scenarios are fictional, they are drawn from composites of real experiences, both positive and negative, that teachers have shared over the years. In the first, we'll see how a colleague advises a high school English teacher to get tough when her attempts to provide quality feedback to students put a burden on her time. In the second scenario, we'll see how a stressed middle school mathematics teacher decides to get even when a student's misbehavior pushes him to his limits. In the third scenario, we'll see how one elementary teacher's recommendation to his colleague to "get real" causes friction and highlights the discrepancies between their well-intentioned, though different, grading policies.

Get Tough

Dr. Kelly Rosewater had been through many cycles in her years of teaching English. She completed her doctorate while working full time, often putting in grueling hours to complete her coursework and dissertation. Although her job did not require it, she frequently wrote articles for professional journals and was the editor of her state association's newsletter. Her dissertation research focused on the importance of feedback for students in English classes. She found that when she provided detailed feedback to students in a timely manner, many of her students appreciated it. At least her very best students appreciated it, and they took her advice to heart. Students often asked her for letters of recommendation for college and job applications, and she was an advisor to the National Honor Society. She devoted her weekends not just to grading student essays but also to providing a paragraph or more of comments on each one. Every year, students who had graduated from college returned to the school to tell Dr. Rosewater how much she had meant to them. These were the days that made her feel that her efforts were not entirely in vain.

But in the past five years or so, Dr. Rosewater noticed a distinct change in the attitudes of many of her students. She always knew that some, perhaps many, students didn't read her comments, but at least they accepted her evaluations as authoritative. Now, however, a growing number of students challenged her evaluations. They would ask rhetorically, "How can you justify this grade?" even though Dr. Rosewater had justified each grade in considerable detail. Her syllabus and grading policies were clear. Student writers were like journalists who had to complete work on deadline or, just as for a newspaper, magazine, or time-critical website, it didn't get reviewed or published. She even gave each student an opt-out twice each semester in order to account for the inevitable illnesses, field trips, and pressures of other classes. While there were ten writing assignments for each semester, students only had to complete eight. Compared to her own experience as a secondary school and university student, Dr. Rosewater was being incredibly understanding, even generous.

But recently, she felt that her generosity had been taken advantage of, with students asking for a third or fourth opt-out, a concession she was unwilling to make. Moreover, the challenges to her grades were growing in intensity, as an increasing number of students would not even talk with her about their grades, but would have their parents send angry and vaguely threatening emails, leave distraught voice mails, and sometimes demand to see her during the school day or after school, times that she had reserved to help students. "How will students learn from feedback," she wondered, "if they don't bother to read it and resist anything except high marks?" Knowing that most students in her classes expected to go to college, she was also concerned that they were going to enter postsecondary education unable to advocate for themselves. Were they going to have their parents call professors? How about job interviewers? How about employers? How helpless were these kids?

Particularly disappointing to Dr. Rosewater was not just the behavior of students and parents but also what she regarded privately as the gutlessness of some of her colleagues and administrators.

"Why go to the trouble?" they told her. "You never win a fight with a student around here, particularly since we've been on the *students are customers* kick."

This analogy particularly offended Dr. Rosewater, as she knew from the experience of her former students that the essence of being a student is delayed gratification—thanking her years after she had offered tough but fair feedback on their work. Customers, on the other hand, sought immediate gratification, and that certainly seemed to be the trend among students and parents.

Although it seemed like a losing battle, Dr. Rosewater was determined not to compromise her professional ethics and personal responsibilities, and therefore she persisted in giving thoughtful, individualized, and specific feedback. She offered the opt-out policy for two assignments per semester but would go no further. The assignments she was to grade had to be turned in on time. She was already strained to the breaking point, and some colleagues' suggestion that she accept late work seemed ludicrous. It simply was not possible to grade any more than the 135 papers that she had been reading every weekend. Additionally, if only 25 percent of those students started taking advantage of a policy accepting late work, she would be attempting to grade more than two hundred essays in a weekend.

Dr. Rosewater therefore resolved to be tough not because she was angry but, as she had learned from her first years of teaching, because she believed strongly in each student's potential and knew that at least someone needed to establish clear expectations and stick to them.

As Dr. Rosewater's frustration betrays, the balance between time and providing quality feedback is a delicate one. Getting tough is one response, and the reflection questions at the end of this chapter will ask you to consider alternatives that allow for effective feedback within the constraints of a reasonable workload. In the next section, we'll take a look at how another teacher experiences and manages his own conflicts within the classroom.

Get Even

Just as there are teachers who are heroic and exceptional, there are teachers who are contemptuous of their students. Even a small number of toxic teachers can have a poisonous influence on the entire school community, as this scenario illustrates.

Mr. Paul Walters was angry. Andrew, the most disruptive student in the middle school, lied to, disrespected, and dared him to get angry. This student was not just disruptive. He was a bully, striding down the hallway with his 190-pound, six-foot frame. While this was unusual for a middle school student, it was not particularly unusual for a sixteen-year-old. Andrew was by far the oldest student in the school, thanks to being held back in third grade (he failed the state's mandatory reading test) and sixth grade (he failed every class and was suspended twice). Mr. Walters took Andrew's taunts until he couldn't take them any longer. In response to every request, command, and plea for order, Andrew responded, "What are you going to do about it? Hit me?" Mr. Walters did not, fortunately, hit the student, but he made sure to ruin him.

Anger had not always been a part of Mr. Walters's personality; he was one of the senior members of the mathematics faculty.

Although, as a former football player and coach, he was certainly intense both in his enthusiasms and in his disappointments, he had earned a reputation as the person who was able to help even the most challenging students through the troubled waters of middle school. When students on the football team failed to meet his academic standards, he had the discretion to remove them, but instead he would collaborate with their classroom teachers, often requiring his students to complete their homework before they could suit up for practice. Whereas some teachers viewed coaches skeptically as people who might protect the eligibility of an athlete at all costs, Coach Walters was known as an ally, not an adversary, of every classroom teacher. Because football was an important part of their identity, few students ever crossed the line with Coach Walters. But mathematics class was a different story. Suspensions and expulsions were extremely rare, even for students who were bullies, who threw books and other items at teachers, and who made the learning environment miserable for everyone involved. Administrators had appreciated Mr. Walters's command of the classroom because he made it a point of pride never to send students to the principal's office for discipline. He knew that he could handle it, and besides, the offenders might think it was a reward to be removed from class. So he persevered, even as Andrew attempted to bully the former coach in the same way that he bullied younger students.

After one particularly depressing day, Mr. Walters was having a beer with a former colleague, Sam Harris, who had retired several years ago. Mr. Harris and Mr. Walters always got along well not only because they were among the minority of men on the middle school faculty but because they shared a professional commitment to students. They had both been coaches, a job that they reckoned paid about fifty cents an hour for all the work they put in. Before they became head coaches, the job paid nothing, even as they worked long hours after school and on weekends with their teams.

"What would you do?" asked Mr. Walters after sharing Andrew's antics for the day.

"What do you think he's like at home?" asked Mr. Harris. Sympathetic to Andrew's home environment, Mr. Walters explained that Andrew's older sister was raising him; both of his parents left home for reasons he didn't entirely understand while Andrew was in elementary school.

"He's sixteen," continued Mr. Harris, "so he might be an emancipated minor. He can make his own decisions about his schooling, including whether to continue his education at all."

"I suppose that's true," Mr. Walters responded tentatively. That night, Mr. Walters slept better than he had in months.

The next day, when Andrew walked in, Mr. Walters exclaimed, "Andrew, it's so great to see you!" Andrew was perplexed at the sudden change in Mr. Walters's demeanor. "I've got an idea I think you're really going to like, so just give me a minute after class, okay?"

Normally, Andrew would have blown off this request from a teacher, and particularly Mr. Walters. But he was intrigued, so he gave Mr. Walters the minute he had requested.

"I've noticed that you seem pretty unhappy, so I wanted to share some news I thought you should know," began Mr. Walters. "You're a young man, sixteen years old, isn't that right?" Andrew nodded.

"Did you know that once you turn sixteen in this state, education is entirely voluntary? Nobody can make you come here anymore, and you can do whatever you'd like. Of course, if you need a letter of recommendation for a job or other school, I'd be happy to provide one. I just thought you'd like to know."

Without saying a word, Andrew gently placed his mathematics book, along with all of his other texts, on the teacher's desk. At least he hadn't thrown it, Mr. Walters thought. And with that, Andrew was out the door and never came back. Teachers started marking Andrew as absent, but after ten unexcused absences, he automatically failed every class. Counselors had tried to call Andrew's older sister about Andrew's absences, but they never were able to get through.

Is Mr. Walter a monster? Is he someone that you cannot even imagine walking the hallways of a school? Although he is a fictional character, he is a composite of real teachers in the real schools where I have worked for decades. He was a good, caring, and decent person—that's what led him to enter the profession in the first place. But years of frustration led him to become a cog in the machine of the dropout factory that was his school. Good people can do awful things, as Mr. Walters surely did. Getting even by sabotaging students and making sure they are ruined are never appropriate responses to the challenges of managing disengaged students, however unpleasant, disruptive, or violent they may be. This scenario is worthy of consideration because it is sometimes easier to have a professional conversation about a fictitious case study than it is about unprofessional behavior within a school. I know of no student who aspires to drop out as Andrew did. But I know of many students who, faced with one too many days of crushing boredom, disrespect, and frustration, walk out the school doors. However troubling this case study may be, I hope that it leads to some productive conversations about how your school will deal with the "Andrews" who are in your classes.

While Andrew's absence from school solves the problems Mr. Walters had with him, getting even and ruining Andrew creates its own set of issues. The reflection questions at the end of this chapter ask you to brainstorm other possible ways to deal with a disruptive student's behavior. In the next section, we turn our attention to a teacher who faces a colleague she considers a bully, and how she deals with his opposing views as they discuss their school's new grading system.

Get Real

Ms. Liz Carlson loved her students, and her students, colleagues, parents, and administrators loved her. She made a point of recognizing every student for academic performance and had artfully constructed a large banner at the front of her class that read, *Everybody Is a Winner!* And she believed it.

"Bless their hearts," she would exclaim. "I've got the best students in the whole world!"

Although her elementary school had adopted a standards-based grading system that was supposed to hold students accountable for their academic performance, old habits were hard to break. For

Ms. Carlson, that meant the new scale was directly related to the previous letter-grade system. All of her students had previously received As or Bs, and in the new system, every student received grades of *exceeds expectations* or *meets expectations*. The other two options of *progressing* or *developing* seemed to Ms. Carlson too close to Cs and Ds, grades she was unwilling to assign to struggling elementary school students. In the few discussions that her colleagues had about grading policies, she was emphatic in her reasoning.

"No student comes to second grade meeting or exceeding expectations. That's what the students are supposed to do at the end of the year. What am I supposed to do? Tell them that they are not okay the minute they walk in the door? I just can't do that."

"Actually, they do come into school not meeting expectations, and it's only fair to tell them that," said the usually quiet Mr. Thurman Moore, a third-grade teacher. "In fact," he continued, "that's why they come to school—to learn to meet expectations. What's the use of grading if we don't tell them the truth?"

Ms. Carlson's voice rose slightly, and she addressed Mr. Moore directly. "Perhaps your third graders are tough enough to handle that sort of criticism, but I can tell you from long experience that the job of a primary-grade teacher is to build the self-esteem of students so that they feel successful in school. That way, I send them to you ready to learn."

"Actually," said Mr. Moore quietly, "many students aren't ready to learn when they come to third grade. We have to get real. These kids have never been told that they need to work harder, ask for help, and understand what they need to do in order to improve. I have to spend a lot of my time in the first semester of third grade teaching second-grade skills because the students have been told that they are fine, but their literacy and mathematics skills are definitely not meeting grade-level standards. Then, I have little time to teach third-grade standards before the tests come in March. It's really discouraging. Every year, I have parents angry with me because they thought that their children were doing great, and the fall report card of third grade was the first time they had any indication that their kids were really not meeting or exceeding expectations. And the administration is not happy about our third-grade test scores."

"You think you can bully kids into higher performance?" asked Ms. Carlson.

"Whoa, hold on," said Alan Simpson, another member of the third-grade team. "Mr. Moore is the most kind and gentle soul I've ever known. He's certainly not a bully, and I'm not sure that sort of language is helpful in this discussion. Telling kids and parents the truth is not mean—it's essential."

"No problem," replied Ms. Carlson. "I'm sorry you thought I called you a bully. You do it your way, and I'll do it mine."

And with that, she rose from the table, poured a cup of coffee, and left the room.

Sometimes, the best way to get along is to agree to disagree. But when it comes to grading policies, inconsistency and unclear expectations can spell disaster for students and teachers alike. As the disagreement between Ms. Carlson and Mr. Moore suggests, getting real about grading is a necessity. But in order for grading to promote student learning effectively, teachers must reconcile personal differences and come to consensus about the grading system they will use and what policies they will implement to support it.

Reflection

The advice to teachers to get tough, get even, and get real has its benefits and drawbacks when addressing students' academic performance and behavior concerns, all of which may affect teachers' abilities to implement effective grading policies that support student learning. Think back on your own experiences in balancing time with providing quality feedback, dealing with disruptive students, and incorporating new grading policies. Then, with your colleagues, reflect on the case studies this chapter presents and answer the following questions to guide your action steps for establishing FAST grading practices in your classroom, school, or district.

1. What is your reaction to the claim that students are customers at Dr. Rosewater's school? How are students similar to customers? How are they different?

2. Think about Dr. Rosewater's feedback practices. How do you believe they would influence student achievement? How do you think students, parents, and fellow faculty members respond to her feedback practices?

3. Dr. Rosewater finds a great deal of affirmation in her former students' testimonials. Have you had similar experiences? How did those visits from former students influence your teaching?

4. Which of Dr. Rosewater's policies would you affirm and perhaps even adopt in your classes? Which policies do you disagree with?

5. Think about your most frustrating experiences with a student, particularly one who was disruptive and potentially violent. How did you respond? If you had the encounters with that student to do over again, how might you respond differently?

6. Consider the emotions, including fear and anger, that Mr. Walters experienced. How would you have coached him to deal with these emotions?

7. If you had Andrew in your class or in your school, how would you have dealt with his behavior as a teacher? How would you have addressed it as an administrator?

8. Put yourself in the position of a parent whose child had Ms. Carlson for a second-grade teacher and Mr. Moore for third grade. Reacting as a parent, not as an educational professional, what do you think about the dialogue that you just read?

9. Many elementary schools, particularly in the primary grades, use descriptive language on report cards rather than

letter grades. Consider the language of the report discussed by Ms. Carlson: *developing, progressing, meets expectations,* and *exceeds expectations.* Think also about the language of the report cards that you use in your school. How could the language of the report cards and the policies about grading be improved to provide better consistency in communicating with students and parents?

10. It's clear that both Ms. Carlson and Mr. Moore love kids and care deeply about them. But they have deep disagreements about teaching, evaluating, and reporting on student progress. If you could take the best qualities of these two teachers, what would they be?

11. If you were an instructional coach or building administrator, what would you have said in the meeting where the conversation between Ms. Carlson and Mr. Moore took place?

Teachers face many challenges in the classroom, from managing heavy grading workloads and addressing student misbehavior to navigating conflicts with colleagues about teaching, grading, and reporting. Addressing these concerns empathetically and with an open mind is an important part of building trust and gaining support for grading reform. Next, part II explores FAST grading as a system that not only promotes student learning from fair, accurate, specific, and timely feedback but also saves teachers time. In chapter 4, we will examine FAST grading practices in depth and learn how schools can establish policies that create consistency and clear expectations.

Part II

Implementing FAST Grading and Improving Best Practices

ESTABLISHING FAST GRADING

In part I, we considered how to build relationships with governing boards, teachers and teachers' unions, parents and guardians, and students. We considered different viewpoints, common opposition to grading reform, and a variety of stakeholder perspectives. Now we turn our attention to the core of this book—how to improve grading policies in a clear and meaningful way. While the specifics of grading systems may vary from one school to another, the essential criteria for effective grading remain the same. Whatever the variation in schools and educational systems, whatever the labels used for grades, every grading policy and practice must be fair, accurate, specific, and timely. In this chapter, we consider the specifics of how to meet these criteria.

FAST Grading

FAST grading provides a wide degree of professional discretion for teachers and administrators. But the essential criteria establish the boundaries within which variation is possible. This is not a new concept for schools. For example, each teacher typically sets class rules, often in collaboration with students. But the value of respect establishes a boundary within which all class rules take place. Specifics, such as respecting the persons and property of classmates, may change in definition, but I don't know of any classroom or school that does not adhere to the fundamental value of respect. Similarly, FAST grading establishes the boundaries of fairness, accuracy, specificity, and timeliness. These boundaries are not a menu but comprise the essential boundaries of effective grading policies. We will consider each of these essentials, and then ask you to reflect on the specific ways in which your class, school, and educational system can establish policies within these boundaries.

Fair

Almost everyone has heard the plaintive cry from students or his or her own children "That's not fair!" more than once. Younger children see their older siblings have later bedtimes and more privileges, and they say, "That's not fair!" Parents patiently explain why additional privileges and responsibilities come with getting older. If, by contrast, we had different rules for twin siblings, it would be a lot more difficult to explain. Similarly, if several students have very similar performances when compared to the academic standards for your school, then those students should receive very similar grades.

Fairness need not be a subjective matter. At the heart of fairness in grading is consistency—the same grade for the same performance when compared to a standard. It may be useful to think of it in athletic terms. If two players hit the basket from the same distance, they earn two points. One might have better attendance at practice, better participation in team discussions, and more diligence in turning in his practice records, but that player still receives only two points for the basket. Coaches have many other ways to give feedback to players about their diligence in practice and other expectations, but coaches don't get to change the rules of the game. That would be unfair.

This is not an argument in favor of dismissing important expectations that teachers have. Rather, the criterion of fairness requires that teachers are precise in how they give feedback to students. Let's explore some common impediments to fairness in grading.

Understanding the Actual Requirements of the Standards

To realize the impact of understanding the actual requirements of standards on ensuring fairness in grading practices, let's examine the sample Common Core and state writing standards for elementary, middle, and high school. Writing is a very high-leverage standard; improvements in writing have a strong influence on improving student performance in reading, mathematics, science, and social studies. Writing is (or should be) required in every class, so it has relevance to every teacher. Please examine the writing standards from figures 4.1, 4.2, and 4.3 (pages 70–71) that align most closely with the grade levels of your classroom or school. Please read with particular care not only what the standards require but also what parts of student performance are *not* in the standards. You will be asked to reflect on your observations after reading the standards.

Common Core State Standards for Fourth-Grade Writing

- **W.4.1:** Write opinion pieces on topics or texts, supporting a point of view with reasons and information.

- **W.4.1a:** Introduce a topic or text clearly, state an opinion, and create an organizational structure in which related ideas are grouped to support the writer's purpose.

- **W.4.1b:** Provide reasons that are supported by facts and details.

- **W.4.1c:** Link opinion and reasons using words and phrases (e.g., for instance, in order to, in addition).

- **W.4.1d:** Provide a concluding statement or section related to the opinion presented.

Source: NGA & CCSSO, 2010.

Figure 4.1: Elementary school writing standards example.

**Texas Essential Knowledge and Skills for English
Language Arts and Reading, Middle School**

Writing and Writing Process

Students use elements of the writing process (planning, drafting, revising, editing, and publishing) to compose text. Students are expected to:

A. Plan a first draft by selecting a genre appropriate for conveying the intended meaning to an audience, determining appropriate topics through a range of strategies (e.g., discussion, background reading, personal interests, interviews), and developing a thesis or controlling idea

B. Develop drafts by choosing an appropriate organizational strategy (e.g., sequence of events, cause-effect, compare-contrast) and building on ideas to create a focused, organized, and coherent piece of writing

C. Revise drafts to clarify meaning, enhance style, include simple and compound sentences, and improve transitions by adding, deleting, combining, and rearranging sentences or larger units of text after rethinking how well questions of purpose, audience, and genre have been addressed

D. Edit drafts for grammar, mechanics, and spelling

E. Revise final draft in response to feedback from peers and teacher and publish written work for appropriate audiences

---

Source: Texas Education Agency, 2015.

Figure 4.2: Middle school writing standards example.

California High School Writing Standards

Text Types and Purposes: (1) Write arguments to support claims in an analysis of substantive topics or texts, using valid reasoning and relevant and sufficient evidence. (2) Write informative/explanatory texts to examine and convey complex ideas and information clearly and accurately through the effective selection, organization, and analysis of content. (3) Write narratives to develop real or imagined experiences or events using effective techniques, well-chosen details, and well-structured event sequences.

Production and Distribution of Writing: (4) Produce clear and coherent writing in which the development, organization, and style are appropriate to task, purpose, and audience. (5) Develop and strengthen writing as needed by planning, revising, editing, rewriting, or trying a new approach. (6) Use technology, including the Internet, to produce and publish writing and to interact and collaborate with others.

Research to Build and Present Knowledge: (7) Conduct short as well as more sustained research projects based on focused questions, demonstrating understanding of the subject under investigation. (8) Gather relevant information from multiple print and digital sources, assess the credibility and accuracy of each source, and integrate the information while avoiding plagiarism. (9) Draw evidence from literary or informational texts to support analysis, reflection, and research.

Range of Writing: (10) Write routinely over extended time frames (time for research, reflection, and revision) and shorter time frames (a single sitting or a day or two) for a range of tasks, purposes, and audiences.

Source: California Department of Education, 2000.

Figure 4.3: High school writing standards example.

After reviewing the standards, please identify in the left column of figure 4.4 the specific skills and knowledge that these standards would imply for your students. In the right column, list the skills and knowledge that are not in these standards.

Knowledge and Skills	Missing Knowledge and Skills

Figure 4.4: Identifying knowledge and skills.

*Visit **go.solution-tree.com/assessment** for a free reproducible version of this figure.*

Identifying the knowledge and skills articulated in the standards is a good first step toward creating shared expectations for learning. But in order to create consistency in a standards-based grading system, teachers who teach the same standards must also share the same expectations about what skills and knowledge students must learn. Shared understanding minimizes chances of unfair or inaccurate grading.

Recognizing How Grading Outside of Standards Hurts Fairness

If we think carefully about the knowledge and skills missing from the standards, we might include those items that teachers think are important enough to influence grades but are not in the standards. A partial list might include the following.

- Working honestly—that is, avoiding plagiarism, copying the work of others, and all other forms of academic dishonesty
- Treating the teacher and fellow students with respect
- Engaging in class discussions
- Turning in homework assignments completely and on time
- Coming to class on time

With this list as a starting point, please list additional expectations in figure 4.5 that you have for students in writing that are not part of the writing standards.

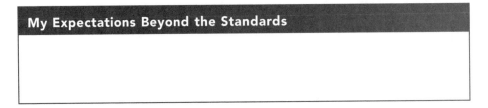

Figure 4.5: Expectations beyond standards.

*Visit **go.solution-tree.com/assessment** for a free reproducible version of this figure.*

There is nothing wrong with establishing these expectations for students. The question is how we apply these expectations to grading. Although almost everyone would agree that expectations beyond the standards are reasonable and appropriate (who is in favor of plagiarism and tardiness?), these expectations can lead to the opposite of fairness. Recall that the essence of fairness is that students with the same performances when compared to the standards will have the same grade. But consider what may happen when educators attempt to incorporate all of their expectations into a single grade.

Mary, Sam, Annika, and Marco all submitted writing that met every standard. In fact, they all submitted written work that clearly exceeded the state standards and the teacher's expectations. Their two co-teachers, Mr. Samir Al-Hokail and Ms. Samantha Allen, provided daily feedback on student work. Here were their grades.

Mary received an A, because she not only had excellent work but also had perfect attendance, engaged actively in class discussions, turned in homework on time, and was clearly the author of her own work.

Sam received a B, despite the fact that his writing was as good as Mary's. Sam and Mary both followed the formula—five paragraphs, clear topic sentences, good transitions, examples and illustrations, and logical conclusions. Sam was often sullen and quiet in class, letting entire class periods go by without a single comment. Even when the teachers called on him, his most frequent reply was "I dunno" or "I'll pass." The teachers believed that the only way to get his attention was to give him a B as a wake-up call.

Annika received a C. Her writing was as good as the compositions from Mary and Sam, but her homework was chronically late. Excellent writing is not enough, the teachers explained, particularly when these students aspired to go to college where they would be expected to get work done on time. The teachers attempted to explain to Annika the value of homework completion, but Annika just shrugged and promised to do better next time.

Marco received a D. His writing was probably the best of the lot, but the teachers ran every essay through a plagiarism detection program and found three paragraphs that were copied, almost word for word, from websites. While Marco vehemently denied the accusation, the teachers were clear that the plagiarism program did not lie. It even showed the websites that matched the text in Marco's essay. Marco's reference list was extensive—the longest of any of the four papers—but it didn't include a citation of these websites for the three paragraphs in question. The teachers' grading policies made very clear that any sort of dishonesty would result in no credit for the assignment, so Marco's essay—stellar in quality—received a zero. His excellent homework, assertive participation in class discussions, and perfect attendance gave the teachers a rationale for not giving him the F that they thought he deserved, but they thought that a D was sufficient punishment for this college-bound student.

The four students about whom you just read all met the same writing standards, and yet they received four different grades. What grades would you have awarded to Mary, Sam, Annika, and Marco? Record the grades and your rationale underlying them in figure 4.6. Please take into consideration your own expectations. How would you include not only student work, but also homework, class participation, and other factors in arriving at your conclusion?

Student	My Grade	Rationale for My Grade
Mary		
Sam		
Annika		
Marco		

Figure 4.6: Determining and rationalizing grades.

Visit go.solution-tree.com/assessment for a free reproducible version of this figure.

Expectations outside of the standards, such as participating in class discussions, submitting assignments on time, and working honestly, can lead to significant distortions in grading policies. Each of these expectations is important enough that it should be called out. Some schools have a report titled "Citizenship and Personal Responsibility" for these items. But it's neither fair nor accurate to call these expectations *writing*. All four students meet the writing standards, with the possible exception of Marco. Sam, Annika, and Marco need feedback to improve their performance, but their written work is stellar. In figure 4.7, record the feedback and appropriate consequences you would suggest to the teacher that do not involve mixing academic and nonacademic performance in the grade.

Student	Feedback and Consequences
Mary	
Sam	
Annika	
Marco	

Figure 4.7: Feedback and consequences for academic and nonacademic performance.

*Visit **go.solution-tree.com/assessment** for a free reproducible version of this figure.*

Professional educators often look at the same student performance and come to very different conclusions about the final grade. Therefore, it's very helpful to ask your colleagues to explain their reasoning. There is no right answer here; the value of the exercise is in understanding how thoughtful, intelligent, and professional colleagues can look at the same student work and come to different conclusions.

Responding to Objections to Fairness in Grading

In the effort to ensure fairness—awarding the same grade for the same performance—educators can incur the wrath of other students and their parents. Consider Mary, who not only had excellent written work, but also met all of the teachers' nonacademic expectations. You can imagine the reaction of Mary and her parents if they discovered that Mary received the same grade as sullen Sam, organizationally challenged Annika, and cheater Marco (who rewrote the essay with appropriate credit for the three paragraphs in question). Mary, in the hunt for class valedictorian, was acutely aware not only of her own grades but also of other students' grades. There were no secrets in high school, even though teachers attempted mightily to keep grades confidential. In a grading system that focuses exclusively on student proficiency, all students receive the same grade. In a grading system that acknowledges behavioral and attitudinal differences among students, each student receives a different grade. If a grading system places teachers on the defensive to explain not only the grade of an individual student but also that student's grade in comparison to other students' grades, then we can expect an increasingly absurd system. In such cases, the addition of even the most trivial variables to a statistically complex formula yields mathematically accurate, yet meaningless, final grades. In this situation, we devalue professional judgment and elevate the ninth decimal point of a grade calculation. The teacher who focuses on student proficiency alone and who therefore awards each of these students the same grade can anticipate some resistance, but the commitment of these teachers to the principles of fairness and accuracy deserves support by their colleagues and administrators.

Responding to students' and parents' concerns about fair grades requires tact and confidentiality. Often, parents and students may feel upset about perceived unfairness, and emotions drive discussions. After all, parents and students are keenly aware grades carry high stakes in determining academic honors, scholarships, and advancement. Although teachers may feel defensive in such discussions with parents and students, they must remain calm. Teachers who clearly articulate their FAST, standards-based grading policy to students and parents at the beginning of the school year open up opportunities for effective communication and minimize chances for misunderstanding and perceptions of unfairness.

To guide your conversations about fairness in grading with parents, students, and other stakeholders, you might refer to the second edition of *Elements of Grading* (Reeves, 2016), where you will find examples of grading practices from a very high-performing school that established clear boundaries for linking grades to performance on academic standards. Homework, for example, accounts for a tiny fraction of the total grade, and it is therefore possible for students to earn an A based on their performance rather than their homework. I spoke with both teachers and instructional coaches in the American International School of Riyadh, and they acknowledge the initial concern that students would simply not do work that did not count toward their final grade. They also worked diligently to create opportunities for practice that were directly related to their summative assessments. Students who participated in those practices, even if it was not part of their grade, performed much better. In brief, a commitment to fairness—scoring students who demonstrate the same performance with the same grade—does not inhibit student responsibility. A commitment to fairness can induce students to work for the right reason—not compliance with teacher demands, but a confident knowledge that their work will improve their performance. With this in mind, consider how you would coach a teacher to respond to students' and parents' concerns about unfairness in grading.

Accurate

Accuracy means that the grade not only is consistent but also measures what we say it does. These requirements reflect the essential components of any assessment. It must be reliable (that is, consistent) and valid (that is, the results reflect what the test purports to measure). Sometimes, the accuracy of grading is simple. Teachers agree that $2 + 5 = 7$. And every teacher who evaluated a student quiz with that equation would agree that this is the correct answer. But a growing number of schools are requiring project-based learning in which teachers are required to give the project a final grade. The same is true of written projects. Sometimes teachers use rubrics, or scoring guides, in order to give a more accurate grade, but it doesn't always work out that way. It is possible that several teachers can look at the identical paper and come to dramatically different conclusions. Grades purport to measure student performance, but mathematical distortions and lack of teacher collaboration in many grading systems undermine accuracy. Let's examine how each of these factors can affect grading.

Mathematical Distortions

We have already addressed one of the greatest mathematical distortions in grading—the use of the zero on a one hundred–point scale. The practical alternative was to revert to a traditional four, three, two, one, zero scale so that students who resolutely refused to turn in work would receive a zero, but at least the zero would be mathematically accurate—that is, there is an equal interval between each grade. The other mathematical distortion in grading policies is the use of the average to compute the final grade. Computers can create the illusion of accuracy because they give meaningless data expressed to three decimal points. Consider three students, each of whom meets the academic standard in his or her summative assessment but receives inaccurate grades because of the use of the average. This is in a school that has a serious commitment to grading reform, having already eliminated the zero on a one hundred–point scale. The teachers have also pledged to ensure fairness in their grading systems by only considering the students' academic work when compared to a standard in awarding grades. But because the school remained locked into a computerized grading system that used the average, the students continued to have inaccurate grades. Each student had ten academic assignments for the term, and each finished the term clearly meeting the standard. In table 4.1, consider the students' grades, reflected on a four–point scale, with A equals 4, B equals 3, C equals 2, D equals 1, and F equals 0.

Table 4.1: Examining Average Grades and Mathematical Distortions of Accuracy

Student	1	2	3
Assignment 1	A	F	A
Assignment 2	A	F	A
Assignment 3	A	F	F
Assignment 4	A	D	F
Assignment 5	A	D	A
Assignment 6	A	C	A
Assignment 7	A	C	F
Assignment 8	A	A	A
Assignment 9	A	A	A
Assignment 10	A	A	A
Final Average	4.0	1.8	2.8

Let's examine how averaging scores may distort accuracy for these three students' grades. With an easy-to-calculate average of 4.0, the first student clearly has earned an A. But what happens to the accuracy of the other two students' final grades when their scores are averaged?

The second student began the semester significantly behind his classmates. Fortunately, the teacher offered exceptional levels of individual support accompanied by consistent and specific feedback. The student then used that feedback to improve performance. While the final scores clearly reflect a strong level of proficiency in meeting the standards, student 2 has an average of 1.8, perhaps a C-minus or D-plus. Think about not only the final performance of student 2, but also the exceptional diligence and work ethic that he displayed. Thanks to the teacher's feedback and his responsible reaction to that feedback, he met the standard with very strong evaluations. But the average made the A impossible and the struggle to attain proficiency seem like a futile endeavor.

The third student was bored. He entered middle school reading at a college level. When he was in school, he was disruptive enough to earn suspensions, and he was frequently out of school because he just didn't show up. He took his academic work seriously—just not all of it. His Fs do not represent poor academic work, but times that he was suspended or absent without excuse. His average is 2.8, and this C-plus represented perhaps the highest grade he had received so far in middle school. With typical adolescent logic, he told his parents and teachers, "Why should I do homework on stuff I already know? Just let me take the test."

Applying your own professional judgment, calculate the final grade for each of these students. Enter your rationale in figure 4.8 (page 80).

Accurate grading systems have grades that reflect student proficiency, and the average actively undermines this. The solution is not a different computer program, but rather supplanting automatic calculations with the professional judgment of teachers. Few teachers who examined only the final grades earned during the marking period would question that all three of these students achieved proficiency and all deserve the same grade of A. But when secondary teachers in particular have 150 students to grade, it's very difficult to take time for a personal judgment call on every one of them. It's frankly easier to just use computerized calculations. That way, they reason, it's not a subjective call by the teacher but an objective report by the computer.

Student	Grade	Rationale
Student 1		
Student 2		
Student 3		

Figure 4.8: Determining and rationalizing accurate grades.

Visit go.solution-tree.com/assessment for a free reproducible version of this figure.

But is the computerized report really objective? The use of the average is a subjective judgment based on the presumption that every student learns in a linear fashion, each taking another step toward meeting the standard at the same time in the same way. This assumption might be accurate for the first student we considered, but it is woefully inaccurate for the others. There are only two ways out of this dilemma. The first is to weight the final grades to account for the vast majority of the student grades—perhaps 80 to 90 percent of the final grade. The common fear to such a solution is that students will just coast until the final weeks of a semester and then, with their grades on the line, will get busy. If that is truly possible, then it's reasonable to ask why the class was designed for thirty-six weeks rather than two. More often, however, students will engage in practice if it is meaningful and related to their final performance. The right kind of practice involves not only performing tasks with which the students are already confident but also attempting different and challenging tasks that will, inevitably, have some errors and failures. The best practice also includes coaching, guidance, and immediate feedback—that is, teacher engagement with students during the practice, not just students' review of feedback days later after papers are graded. The second way out of the dilemma is to embrace the teacher's professional judgment regarding each student's proficiency. This judgment might be informed by the data, but it not bound by it. The Advanced Placement statistics teacher knows that the average—the arithmetic mean—is not the best representation of a data set. The remedial English teacher knows the same. In both cases, their professional judgment relies on their observations as teachers rather than on grade entries in a database to recognize the proficiency level students attain.

Supplanting the average with teacher judgment and heavy weighting of the final tasks is one step toward accuracy. The second step is improved teacher collaboration.

Lack of Teacher Collaboration

Just as computer-generated averages generate the illusion of precision and objectivity, teacher-graded performance tasks (particularly in work such as writing) are often regarded as inherently subjective. I once asked a teacher what the criteria were for evaluating students and, pointing to his head, he proudly said, "It's right here." I was not surprised when I asked the principal how she evaluated teachers, and her response was nearly identical. There was no rubric or scoring guide for teachers, because she had it all, pointing to her head, "right up here."

Unfortunately, this lack of shared criteria for evaluation is all too common and can lead to some significant challenges in establishing FAST grading practices. To examine how inaccuracies in assessment and grading may arise when there is a lack of teacher collaboration, try this exercise yourself with a group of colleagues, including teachers and administrators. Divide the participants in this exercise into three groups of roughly equal size, group A, group B, and group C. All groups will assess the same student writing sample (see figure 4.9, pages 82–83). Sixth-grade students were allowed to choose a topic and then write a persuasive essay, using evidence and arguments to support their points of view. Group A will use the rubric in figure 4.10 (pages 84–87), group B will use the rubric in figure 4.11 (pages 88–89), and group C will use the rubric in figure 4.12 (pages 90–91) to assess the writing sample.

Topic: Persuade your principal that school should start one hour later.

There are so many things about middle school that I have had to get used to. The hardest thing for me has been getting up earlier than I did in elementary school. Everyone knows that kids need their sleep, and if we don't get enough, then we get cranky. Because of this, I think it should be considered that school starts one hour later.

Being able to get more sleep is only one of the reasons school should start later. If I want to get the recommended nine hours of sleep to be ready for school in the morning, then that means I have to be asleep by 10:00 at night. Yeah right! That never happens. For us kids who play sports after school, we don't usually get home until 5:00 or 6:00 at night. Sometimes it's even later. Then once we get home we have to eat dinner, bathe, and do homework. That doesn't leave much time to get to bed by 10:00. Plus, I'm only in sixth grade, so it's probably even more difficult for the eighth graders. I would suggest switching our early start time with the elementary school start time. Those younger kids are usually up early anyways! If we were able to come to school one hour later, we would be able to get more sleep and be less stressed at night about going to bed early.

A second reason why school should start an hour later is it would give us more time to eat breakfast at home (or at school) in the morning. Isn't breakfast the most important meal of the day? Breakfast is what gives me my energy in the morning to stay awake and learn at school. If we had an extra hour in the morning, then we could have an even better breakfast than the usual grab a granola bar for the car and run out the door. I don't even like granola bars, but I love breakfast, and I would love to be able to eat a better meal in the morning.

> My last reason would be good for our school. Because school starts early, I always see kids running into school and needing to get a tardy slip from the door monitor. Sometimes, it is not even their fault because the drop-off line is so long in the morning. If school started one hour later, then I bet there would be fewer tardy kids, and that would make our school look better. Not only that, but then kids wouldn't be coming into class late and missing part of the teacher's lesson. The teachers hate that.
>
> It is very clear to me, and I hope it is to you too, that school should start an hour later. We would be able to get more sleep, eat a better breakfast, and have fewer tardies on our records. When we are in school, we need to be awake and able to learn, and I think starting school later would help us do that. After all, we are still growing kids! I hope you consider my reasons and that middle school will eventually start later.

Figure 4.9: Student writing sample.

Once copies of the sample student writing and the appropriate rubrics are distributed to each group, follow these four steps.

1. Every person on each team should evaluate the writing example entirely alone and without collaboration with a partner. Show your individual score here: _____

2. Using its assigned rubric, each group should collaborate to determine a final grade for the writing sample. No pluses or minuses are allowed—just the grade that best fits the group's assigned rubric. Enter it here: _____

3. All teams convene as one large group to discuss their final scores and why they arrived at their score.

4. All teams identify the strengths and weaknesses of the rubrics they used, and then collectively determine the criteria appropriate for a schoolwide rubric for sixth-grade persuasive writing.

	4 (Above Grade Level)	3 (At Grade Level)	2 (Approaching Grade Level)	1 (Below Grade Level)
Focus and Opinion CCSS: • W.1a • W.1b • W.4	• Responds skillfully to all parts of the prompt • States an argument, claim, or opinion that demonstrates an insightful understanding of topic or text	• Responds to all parts of the prompt • States an argument, claim, or opinion that demonstrates an understanding of topic or text	• Responds to most parts of the prompt • States an argument, claim, or opinion that demonstrates limited understanding of topic or text	• Responds to some or no parts of the prompt • Does not state an opinion or demonstrates little to no understanding of topic or text
Organization CCSS: • W.1a • W.1c • W.1d • W.4	• Organizes ideas and information into purposeful, coherent paragraphs that include an elaborated introduction with clear thesis, structured body, and insightful conclusion • Uses a variety of linking words, phrases, and clauses skillfully to connect reasons to argument, claim, or opinion	• Organizes ideas and information into logical introductory, body, and concluding paragraphs • Uses linking words, phrases, and clauses appropriately to connect reasons to argument, claim, or opinion	• Organizes ideas and information in an attempted paragraph structure that includes a sense of introduction, body, and conclusion • Uses some linking words, phrases, or clauses to connect reasons to argument, claim, or opinion but simplistically	• Does not organize ideas and information coherently due to lack of paragraph structure or a missing introduction, body, or conclusion • Uses no linking words, phrases, or clauses

	4 (Above Grade Level)	3 (At Grade Level)	2 (Approaching Grade Level)	1 (Below Grade Level)
Support and Evidence **CCSS:** • **RI.1** • **W.1b** • **W.9b**	• Supports opinion skillfully with substantial and relevant evidence • Provides insightful explanation or analysis of how evidence supports claims	• Supports opinion with sufficient and relevant evidence • Provides clear explanation or analysis of how evidence supports claims	• Supports opinion with limited or superficial evidence • Provides some explanation or analysis of how evidence supports claims	• Does not support opinion with evidence or evidence is irrelevant or inaccurate • Provides no or inaccurate explanation or analysis of how evidence supports claims
Language **CCSS:** • **L.1** • **L.2**	• Uses purposeful and varied sentence structures • Demonstrates creativity and flexibility when using conventions (grammar, punctuation, capitalization, and spelling) to enhance meaning • Uses precise and sophisticated academic and domain-specific vocabulary appropriate for the audience and purpose	• Uses correct and varied sentence structures • Demonstrates grade-level-appropriate conventions; errors are minor and do not obscure meaning • Uses academic and domain-specific vocabulary appropriate for the audience and purpose	• Uses some repetitive yet correct sentence structures • Demonstrates some grade-level-appropriate conventions, but errors obscure meaning • Uses limited academic and/or domain-specific vocabulary for the audience and purpose	• Does not demonstrate sentence mastery • Demonstrates limited understanding of grade-level-appropriate conventions, and errors interfere with the meaning • Uses no academic or domain-specific vocabulary

continued on next page →

Strand	Fifth Grade	Sixth Grade	Seventh Grade
Writing	**W.5.1.** Write opinion pieces on topics or texts, supporting a point of view with reasons and information.	**W.6.1.** Write arguments to support claims with clear reasons and relevant evidence.	**W.7.1.** Write arguments to support claims with clear reasons and relevant evidence.
	W.5.1a. Introduce a topic or text clearly, state an opinion, and create an organizational structure in which ideas are logically grouped to support the writer's purpose.	**W.6.1a.** Introduce claims and organize the reasons and evidence clearly.	**W.7.1a.** Introduce claims, acknowledge alternate or opposing claims, and organize the reasons and evidence logically.
	W.5.1b. Provide logically ordered reasons that are supported by facts and details.	**W.6.1b.** Support claims with clear reasons and relevant evidence, using credible sources and demonstrating an understanding of the topic or text.	**W.7.1b.** Support claims with logical reasoning and relevant evidence, using accurate, credible sources and demonstrating an understanding of the topic or text.
	W.5.1c. Link opinion and reasons using words, phrases, and clauses (such as consequently, specifically, and so on).	**W.6.1c.** Use words, phrases, and clauses to clarify the relationships among claims and reasons.	**W.7.1c.** Use words, phrases, and clauses to create cohesion and clarify the relationships among claims, reasons, and evidence.
	W.5.1d. Provide a concluding statement or section related to the opinion presented.	**W.6.1d.** Establish and maintain a formal style.	**W.7.1d.** Establish and maintain a formal style.
		W.6.1e. Provide a concluding statement or section that follows from the argument presented.	**W.7.1e.** Provide a concluding statement or section that follows from and supports the argument presented.
	W.5.4. Produce clear and coherent writing (including multiparagraph texts) in which the development and organization are appropriate to task, purpose, and audience.	**W.6.4.** Produce clear and coherent writing in which the development, organization, and style are appropriate to task, purpose, and audience.	**W.7.4.** Produce clear and coherent writing in which the development, organization, and style are appropriate to task, purpose, and audience.

Strand	Fifth Grade	Sixth Grade	Seventh Grade
	W.5.9. Draw evidence from literary or informational texts to support analysis, reflection, and research.	**W.6.9.** Draw evidence from literary or informational texts to support analysis, reflection, and research.	**W.7.9.** Draw evidence from literary or informational texts to support analysis, reflection, and research.
Reading—Informational Text	**RI.5.1.** Quote accurately from a text when explaining what the text says explicitly and when drawing inferences from the text.	**RI.6.1.** Cite textual evidence to support analysis of what the text says explicitly as well as inferences drawn from the text.	**RI.7.1.** Cite several pieces of textual evidence to support analysis of what the text says explicitly as well as inferences drawn from the text.
Language	**L.5.1.** Demonstrate command of the conventions of standard English grammar and usage when writing or speaking.	**L.6.1.** Demonstrate command of the conventions of standard English grammar and usage when writing or speaking.	**L.7.1.** Demonstrate command of the conventions of standard English grammar and usage when writing or speaking.
	L.5.2. Demonstrate command of the conventions of standard English capitalization, punctuation, and spelling when writing.	**L.6.2.** Demonstrate command of the conventions of standard English capitalization, punctuation, and spelling when writing.	**L.7.2.** Demonstrate command of the conventions of standard English capitalization, punctuation, and spelling when writing.

Sources: Elk Grove Unified School District; NGA & CCSSO, 2010. Used with permission.

Figure 4.10: Sixth-grade opinion and argumentative writing rubric (use with group A).

Notes: The criterion boxes on the left of the rubric identify the California Common Core–aligned standards. As a resource for teachers, this figure shows the sixth-grade standards, as well as those for the preceding and subsequent grades.

W = Writing   RI = Reading—Informational Text   L = Language

*Visit **go.solution-tree.com/assessment** for a free reproducible version of this figure.*

Sixth-Grade Writing Rubric

	Ideas and Content (Ideas)	Organization	Style (Voice, Word Choice, Fluency)	Language Conventions	Points
6 Exceeds Standards	Stays on the topic (does not ramble or repeat) Includes main ideas with four or more well-developed supporting details Includes in-depth information and exceptional, fully developed supporting details Creates clear and vivid images for reader that go beyond the obvious or predictable Uses original ideas that reflect insight	Shows mastery of multiple-paragraph form Has an engaging introduction and satisfying conclusion Has a clear sequence that enhances meaning with a beginning, middle, and end Uses effective, varied, and thoughtful transitions between sentences and paragraphs Uses well-controlled pacing	Includes dynamic, vivid, or challenging words, enhancing meaning and clarifying understanding and adding energy and depth Uses original, unique, authoritative or interesting voice Uses purposeful and varied sentence beginnings that add variety and energy Has complete, complex sentences varying in length and structure Uses literary devices very effectively Has fluent writing with cadence	Few or no errors in capitalization Few or no errors in punctuation Few or no errors in subject and verb agreement Few or no errors in the spelling of grade-level-appropriate words Few or no run-on sentences or sentence fragments Indention of paragraphs all of the time	4
5 Exceeds Standards	Stays on the topic (does not ramble or repeat) Includes main ideas with four or more developed supporting details Includes in-depth information and exceptional, fully developed supporting details Creates clear and vivid images for reader Uses original ideas	Shows understanding of multiple-paragraph form Has an inviting introduction and conclusion Has a clear sequence with a beginning, middle, and end Uses effective and varied transitions between sentences and paragraphs	Includes dynamic, vivid or challenging words, enhancing meaning and clarifying understanding Uses original, unique, authoritative, or interesting voice Has a variety of complete, complex sentences Uses literary devices effectively Has fluent writing	
4 Meets Standards	Stays on the topic (does not ramble or repeat) Includes main ideas with three or more developed supporting details Creates images for reader	Shows understanding of multiple-paragraph form Has an effective introduction and conclusion Has a clear sequence with a beginning, middle, and end	Includes some dynamic, vivid, or challenging words Uses literary devices Uses original, unique, authoritative, or interesting voice Uses complete, complex sentences	Most capitalization is correct Indention of paragraphs all of the time Most sentences contain correct punctuation Most sentences use appropriate verb tense Most sentences have correct subject and verb agreement	3

	Uses effective transitions between sentences and paragraphs	Has fluent writing	Most grade-level words are spelled correctly / Few or no run-on sentences or sentence fragments	
3 Below Standards	Shows understanding of paragraph form Has an identifiable introduction and conclusion Has a logical progression of main ideas and supporting details—has a beginning, middle, and end Attempts transitions between sentences and paragraphs	Uses basic vocabulary appropriately Attempts to use literary devices Demonstrates an awareness of audience Uses simple effective sentence patterns	Some capitalization is correct Some sentences have correct punctuation Some sentences have correct subject and verb agreement Some grade-level-appropriate words spelled correctly Some run-on sentences or sentence fragments Indention of paragraphs most of the time	2
2 Below Standards	Shows some understanding of paragraph forms Lacks introduction or conclusion Has limited sequence of events (may include only one of the elements: beginning, middle, or end) Attempts few transitions	Uses basic vocabulary appropriately most of the time Demonstrates little awareness of audience		
1 Below Standards	Does not attempt paragraph form Lacks introduction or conclusion Has limited sequence of events (may include only one of the elements: beginning, middle, or end) Attempts no transitions	Uses limited basic vocabulary, uses some words inappropriately Attempts simple sentence patterns but not understandable Demonstrates little or no awareness of audience	Many errors in capitalization Punctuation missing or incorrect Many errors in subject and verb agreement Many errors in spelling Many run-on sentences or fragments Indention of paragraphs nonexistent	1

Figure 4.11: Sixth-grade writing rubric (use with group B).

Visit go.solution-tree.com/assessment for a free reproducible version of this figure.

Trait	4	3	2	1	Points Earned	Comments
Ideas	Ideas are well developed and supported by details. Thesis is clearly stated. Primary and secondary ideas are tied to and support thesis.	Ideas are developed and supported by details. Thesis is clearly stated. Primary and secondary ideas are relevant and try to support thesis.	Ideas are presented and explained. Thesis is stated but may be unclear. Primary and secondary ideas are present and clearly stated.	Ideas are presented but not explained well. Thesis is unclear. Primary and secondary ideas are unclear or may not be present at all.		
Organization	Correct form is used and enhances the writing. Ideas are grouped together, are tied to thesis, and enhance meaning. Transitions work well.	Correct form is used. Ideas are grouped together and attempt to enhance meaning. Transitions are basic but clear.	Correct form is used. Ideas are grouped together. Transitions need improvement.	Form is obvious, but not entirely correct. Ideas are scattered throughout with no real coherence. Transitions are missing.		
Voice	Voice of the author is able to engage the audience, and consistent throughout the writing.	Voice of the author is able to engage the audience throughout most of the writing, but changes once or twice.	Voice of the author is somewhat engaging and somewhat clear, but changes throughout the work for no reason.	Voice of the author is unclear, but there is an attempt at engaging the audience.		

Trait	4	3	2	1	Points Earned	Comments
	Voice is clear and fitting for the type of writing and shows personality of author.	Voice is clear but does not entirely fit the piece.	—	The audience is rarely engaged.		
Support and Evidence	The author provides well-developed and accurate support for the opinion, or personal preference. The author provides insightful explanation and analysis of how evidence supports claims.	The author provides accurate and sufficient support for the opinion or personal preference. The author provides clear explanation and analysis of how evidence supports claims.	The author provides some inaccurate support for the opinion or personal preference. The author provides some explanation and analysis of how evidence supports claims.	The author provides little accurate support for the opinion or personal preference. The author provides no or inaccurate explanation and analysis of how evidence supports claims.		
Conventions	Strong use of conventions makes writing meaningful and easy to read. There are few or no errors.	Some mistakes in grammar, spelling, or punctuation, but meaning is still clear.	Many errors in all areas of conventions. Errors get in the way of meaning.	Many errors in word usage, mechanics, spelling, and sentence structure make meaning unclear to the audience.		

Points Earned _____   Points Possible _____

Sources: Elk Grove Unified School District. Used with permission.

Figure 4.12: Sixth-grade persuasive writing rubric (use with group C).

Visit go.solution-tree.com/assessment for a free reproducible version of this figure.

This is a particularly important exercise. The recognition that, despite rubrics, we all tend to evaluate students in different ways is an important acknowledgment of professional differences. It's not a moral or professional weakness, but simply recognition of reality.

Certainly, the same is true of letter grades. In experiments with more than ten thousand teachers and administrators (Reeves, 2012), participants were asked, "What's the difference between a student who earns As and Bs and the student who earns Ds and Fs?" The responses are very consistent—the A and B students are:

- More responsible
- More engaged
- More likely to receive assistance from parents
- More intelligent
- Better at taking tests
- Less likely to use drugs
- Willing to follow the rules
- Organized enough to get their work done on time
- Willing to talk with the teacher when they need help

At this point, I ask all the participants to work entirely alone to grade a single student. The student had some high marks, especially at the end of the term, but also had some low marks and several missing assignments. Specifically, the student's marks in the order they were received were:

- C
- C
- MA (missing assignment)
- D
- C
- B
- MA
- MA

- B
- A

Try it—what grade would you award to this student? The results with thousands of teachers were astonishing. The same student received these grades from teachers:

- A—7 percent
- B—13 percent
- C—39 percent
- D—21 percent
- F—20 percent

It's important to note that the following characteristics did not change for the student.

- Level of responsibility
- Level of engagement
- Level of assistance from parents
- Intelligence
- Willingness to follow the rules
- Level of organization
- Level of getting work done
- Willingness to talk with the teacher when in need of help

The only explanation for the differences in the letter grades was the individual teacher's idiosyncratic grading policies. If there were a source of outrage in your community, then it ought to be the mystery surrounding grading. Imagine you are a parent and one of your children was awarded grades from three teachers, all of whom agreed exactly about your child's intelligence, organization, and test performance. Now imagine how you would react if one teacher awarded him or her an A, another a C, and another an F. You would rightfully be outraged. But in actual practice, the real parental outrage is often reserved for any changes in grading systems.

Collaboration can be an effective antidote to subjectivity in areas ranging from the assessment of primary students to the evaluations of teachers and administrators. Effective collaboration requires three elements. First, there must be a clear statement of expectations of performance. This usually involves a rubric, often on a four–point scale that might have labels such as *developing, progressing, proficient*, and *exemplary*. The second requirement is that teachers and administrators engage in systematic collaboration to test the accuracy of their evaluations. For example, when five teachers look at the same piece of student work, at least four out of the five should conclude, working independently, that the student achieved the same score. When that is not the case, the teachers each discuss their personal rationale for the grade, and the group will quickly see if it can achieve consensus. If the members cannot, then it's important to remember this rule of collaboration: the enemy is not one another; the enemy is ambiguity. Therefore, the group works together to reduce the ambiguity and improve the clarity of the rubric so that the teachers agree more easily on what the score of a piece of student work will be. The third requirement for effective collaboration is a system for reducing future ambiguities and disagreements. One reason that genuine collaboration is rare among teachers is that it is so frustratingly difficult and, in many cases, collaboration leaves teachers exhausted and angry, no closer to their objective than when they started. The cultural barrier in schools that is the most impervious to change is the teacher's ability to exercise control within the four walls of the classroom. Therefore, the third and most important requirement for collaboration is what DuFour (2015) has incisively described as public practice. In no other profession worthy of its name is it regarded as acceptable for practitioners to define their own results without any deference to the judgment of colleagues.

This is precisely what teachers expect when administrators evaluate them. It is infuriating for teachers when they receive different—even contradictory—feedback from evaluators. Despite the deluge of teacher evaluation instruments, the evaluators' inconsistent applications of them is appalling. Teachers spend hours in many systems building a portfolio of their accomplishments, sometimes in binders, sometimes in elaborate computer record-keeping systems. They are often working without models, with only a bewildering array of inconsistent expectations and requirements. Overwhelmed administrators defer observations until they have a day without discipline problems, parent complaints, and staff conflicts to manage. That is to say, the administrators engage in observations after it is too late to do anything about what they see. Teachers find these deeply flawed evaluation processes not only unfair but inaccurate. Teachers know that judgments about their performance can be specific, clear, and consistent. They also know that their ability to improve throughout the year should be reflected in their evaluations, but for systems that average the results of every evaluation, teachers are punished in the spring for the errors of the fall. When it comes to accuracy in grading, we must provide at least the same commitment to student evaluation as we expect for teacher evaluation. That means clarity, consistency, and professional judgment—not bizarre collections of materials that are evaluated without collaboration and in an inconsistent manner.

Specific

Teachers are caught in a difficult bind when they attempt to improve the specificity of their grading practices. There are far too many academic standards, particularly for schools that expect teachers to close the gap of several years of academic ineffectiveness during a single academic year. At the same time, there are too few standards because teachers know that standards such as personal organization, project management, time management, the ability to ask for assistance, and the ability to receive and apply feedback are never articulated in lists of academic standards, yet are critically important for student success. This can lead to two extremes, with one extreme representing the use of a single grade to represent student performance. The other extreme is the use of a catalog of standards, requiring students to include performance in a dozen or more areas on the report card. This leads to report cards that are many pages long, often in very tiny fonts. Certainly, students require more than a single letter or number to understand the teacher's evaluation of their performance, but they also need a report card that they will take the time to read.

The answer to this dilemma is what I call *power standards* (Reeves, 2005). This subset of standards meets three requirements. The first is leverage—that is, the standard has applicability in a variety of disciplines and the school. For example, the writing standards that we considered in figures 4.1, 4.2, and 4.3 (pages 69–71) clearly have leverage, because writing is required in science, social studies, and mathematics. In great schools, writing is required in every subject and every grade. The second requirement for power standards is that they have endurance. By endurance, I mean that the same standard is required across grade levels for years to come. When teachers review standards, they should not only consider the academic expectations but also look at the requirements for their students for years into the future. The third requirement for power standards is based on the question, What is essential for the next level of learning? For example, if you are teaching fourth grade, it is very helpful to ask a fifth-grade teacher, "What must my students be able to know and do in order to enter your class next year with confidence and success?" I have never had the teacher in the next-higher grade respond that students must know every single standard. Rather, he or she gives a concise and focused list. This list typically includes only the most important academic standards and skills not listed in the standards, such as organizational ability and the willingness to ask for help. This intergrade dialogue should be included as part of any grading reform effort, as the audience for grades is not only students and parents but also teachers in the next grade level.

Timely

For grades and other feedback to be timely, teachers must provide them quickly enough for students to apply the feedback and teachers to improve instruction. For example, at Adlai Stevenson High School, the initial interval between grading periods was initially nine weeks, fairly typical for secondary schools. The problem was that if a student was not doing well early in the semester, more than two months elapsed before the student received a grade, rendering the feedback almost useless. This is particularly true if the final semester grade was calculated by averaging the grades of the two grading periods within each semester. A student who fails the first term, but finally begins to understand and learn in the second term and earns an A, will at best have a C for the final grade. So consider what Adlai Stevenson High School administrators did (DuFour et al., 2010). They changed the interval for grades from nine weeks to six weeks, and teachers agreed in the middle of each grading period— that is, every three weeks—to provide feedback to students on their grades. If at the end of the three-week feedback period a student was not doing well, the teachers and other students provided one-to-one assistance to get the student back on track for success. The impact was dramatic, reducing course failure rates and increasing graduation rates from 65 percent to almost 100 percent.

Even the best and most sophisticated feedback is rendered impotent if it is not delivered in a timely manner. Consider the greatest complaint that teachers have about student testing. Even when the tests are well designed and related to the curriculum, it doesn't help the teachers to give feedback to students and improve their teaching practice if the results are not released until after the students have left school. This is the typical state of affairs when tests are administrated late in the school year, scores are announced in the following year, and teachers are expected to engage in data-driven decision making for instructional strategies directed at students who are no longer in their classrooms. Administrators are unable to design relevant school improvement plans in the summer if they don't have results until the fall. If we find these delays in feedback frustrating, then we must avoid making the same mistake with students.

Reflection

The following six exercises in this chapter are important first steps. They demonstrate that the grading system is broken because the same student with the same performance can have very different grades depending on which scoring guide or grading policy is used. In a word, these systems are unfair—contrary to the first criterion of FAST grading. And when the game isn't fair, students simply stop playing the game.

1. Consider how your expectations outside of standards may lead to grading distortions. In figure 4.13, identify your expectations and with colleagues, discuss how these criteria may contribute to unfairness in grading. What biases or challenges did your colleagues uncover that you didn't expect?

Expectations	Potential Biases or Challenges to Fair Grading

Figure 4.13: Uncovering biases and challenges of expectations outside standards.

*Visit **go.solution-tree.com/assessment** for a free reproducible version of this figure.*

2. Accuracy in grading, just like accuracy in teacher evaluation, requires teacher judgment and effective collaboration. In figure 4.14, consider one of your grading practices and identify ways in which you could improve accuracy. For example, if your computer uses the average, you might want to put in the right column that you would remove the default to the average, increase the weight of summative assessments in calculating the final grade, and add a review for teacher professional judgment for any grade lower than a B.

Grading Practice	Improved Accuracy

Figure 4.14: Considerations for improving accuracy of grading practices.

*Visit **go.solution-tree.com/assessment** for a free reproducible version of this figure.*

3. What conclusions do you draw from the results of your scoring of student writing? Consider ways in which you

might achieve a greater degree of consistency in scoring student work, including the following.

- ◊ Improving the specificity of the rubric
- ◊ Practicing scoring with additional pieces of student work
- ◊ Expressing the rubric in student-accessible language
- ◊ Including students in the scoring process so that they better understand how they are assessed
- ◊ Sharing other ideas you have for improving the consistency of scoring

4. Consider the different ways that you and your colleagues responded to the exercise on calculating the final grade for the same student with the identical performance. What accounted for the differences from one teacher to another?

5. Consider the standards for a specific subject in your grade level. Please use the academic standards that are directly relevant to your jurisdiction. In the left-hand column of figure 4.15, write those standards. In the right-hand column, narrow the focus to the power standards—those standards that provide leverage and endurance and are most necessary for the next level of instruction.

In completing this exercise, be mindful of the paradox of standards—that is, there are simultaneously too many of them and too few of them.

Standards	Power Standards

Figure 4.15: Identifying power standards to improve specificity.

*Visit **go.solution-tree.com/assessment** for a free reproducible version of this figure.*

6. In figure 4.16 (page 100), consider ways that you can improve the timeliness of feedback and grades that you

provide to students. In particular, consider the intervals between releasing report cards, giving timely feedback to those students (and their parents) who are not meeting standards, and incorporating daily feedback to students.

Feedback Strategy	Methods to Improve Timeliness
Interval Between Report Cards	
Feedback for Students Not Meeting Standards	
Daily Feedback to Students	
Additional Feedback Strategies	

Figure 4.16: Considerations for improving timeliness of feedback.

*Visit **go.solution-tree.com/assessment** for a free reproducible version of this figure.*

FAST grading benefits students and teachers alike. Fair, accurate, specific, and timely feedback helps to ensure that teachers keep the objective of improving student learning at the forefront of their grading practices. Chapter 5 provides strategies to support a FAST grading system and save busy teachers time.

Chapter 5

IMPLEMENTING TIME-SAVING STRATEGIES FOR BUSY TEACHERS

When I ask teachers the number-one reason that they can't implement new ideas, however promising, the consistent answer is "We don't have the time!" It's not money, administrative support, or other factors. The overwhelming complaint of teachers is that there is too much to do in too short a period of time. In this chapter, we will consider the causes of the teacher time crunch, how poor grading practices cost teachers time, and how improved grading practices can save time.

Why Teachers Are Crunched for Time

I've interviewed teachers around the world and found some very consistent analyses of the causes of their anxiety over the limited amount of time available to them. These interviews include teachers in public and independent schools throughout North America and more than twenty other countries. Whether they follow traditional schedules, block schedules, full-day schedules, morning-only schedules, or alternative schedules (such as schools that begin their first class at four o'clock in the afternoon), the primary concern remains the same: too many standards and too much curriculum and not enough time. Teachers state that one of their primary concerns is that academic expectations exceed the amount of time available.

I've found this to be the case from kindergarten through secondary school. Governing authorities mean well when they establish standards. These documents are not perfect, but surely they are better than the bad old days of curriculum chaos. Despite these good intentions, even the most focused standards make the assumption that every student requires only one year of learning to understand and demonstrate proficiency in these standards. The fact is that many students require more than one year of learning. At the secondary level, the curriculum has expanded dramatically, even though the hours allocated to subjects remain the same as in the 1970s. Consider, for example, the developments in biology, chemistry, European history, and U.S. history. Unless history stopped at the Vietnam War or before the advent of biochemical engineering, then giving teachers in these subjects the same amount of time now must depend on the presumptions that teachers can talk very quickly to cover the content, and that students can listen to lectures more quickly. This is an unwise conclusion. Teachers are perfectly capable of teaching their subjects, but given the expanded curriculum demands, they need more time. Many secondary classes could be expanded to two years or two periods within the same year. At every grade level, teachers must be able to identify the power standards rather than engage in the futile drill of coverage.

How Poor Grading Practices Cost Teachers Time

Although teachers and administrators are acutely aware of the pressures of time, they sometimes persist in practices that cost them extra time. For example, it might appear on the surface that "no retake" and "no late work" policies would save teachers time. Some have understandable concerns that if students are allowed to submit late work or retake tests, they will overwhelm the teacher with numerous assignments to grade during the last week of school, when teachers are already overloaded with end-of-year report cards, self-evaluations, goal setting, and other requirements. Teachers are also understandably concerned that a failure to rely on automatically calculated grades in a computerized grading system will place an additional burden on their limited time. Although teachers may initially spend less time grading if they use a computerized system, they will find that automatic grade calculations will cost them—and students—a significant amount of time and effort down the road. Let's survey the real costs of maintaining traditional grading policies and how such policies promote failure.

In previous chapters, we established clearly that grading policies that assume every student learns at the same rate and at the same time are not based in reality. Moreover, policies that assume all homework should be done outside of class do not conform to the best-available research about practice, feedback, and improvement as a means to achieve better student performance (Hattie, 2012; Marzano, 2000). We also know that the default to the computerized average demotivates students, makes them less likely to respect teacher feedback, and inaccurately escalates the failure rate. In sum, any grading policy that increases the failure rate may appear to save time but in fact costs time.

Envision, if you will, the cost of failure. At the very least, failing students become discipline problems at the end of the semester, distracting other students and teachers from their essential work. Students who repeat a class are older than their peers and find doing the same class over again an exercise in futility. Teachers find repeaters a threat to classroom order and a distraction from their professional responsibilities. What about failing students who don't cause disruptions and don't repeat classes? We have a technical name for them—they are called dropouts.

Many states have convoluted ways of calculating the dropout rate, but the easiest way to evaluate the dropout situation in your school is to compare the size of the ninth-grade class to the size of the senior class. Some schools take pride in the fact that, after years of disappointment, the average scores of their juniors and seniors increase. Sometimes that is true because the lowest-performing students are no longer there. When the student population decreases, opportunities for expanding the teaching force decreases. Opportunities for teachers to provide interesting and creative elective classes decrease. Grading practices that increase failures and dropouts do not save the time of teachers but only serve to increase their burdens in future years. For example, students who fail ninth-grade mathematics and science classes—often the courses with the highest failure rates in high schools—are required to repeat those ninth-grade classes during their second year of high school. Teachers then face the unpleasant task of dealing with angry, demotivated, and self-described "failures" who are sixteen years old and sitting next to their fourteen-year-old classmates. Moreover, the cost of repeaters and dropouts on teacher morale and community support is devastating. The Alliance for Excellent Education (2015) documents the cost of dropouts with regard to medical care, tax revenue, and involvement in the criminal justice system. There is simply no defense for a policy that increases the dropout rate.

It is certainly true that providing effective feedback, engaging in collaborate scoring, and ensuring that nonproficient students get the support they need all take time. But the most unsustainable practice is to expect a continuation of the system in which teachers spend an extraordinary amount of their evening and weekend time engaged in traditional grading practices. Specifically, these hardworking teachers grade papers that students will not have the opportunity to resubmit, make comments on essays, lab reports, and mathematics problems that students do not read, and admonish students to improve their work habits long after it is too late for the students to influence their final grades. While these practices may seem appropriate for the lone heroic teacher who works to the point of exhaustion, they are unsustainable. What is necessary is to provide time within the school day. In the next section, we'll see how improved grading practices during the school day shift teachers' burdens away from grading the most assignments during the final and most chaotic week of the school year to being spread throughout the year.

How Improved Grading Practices Save Teachers Time

Let's consider the flip side of the coin. How do improved grading practices save teachers time? Consider the case of homework. When it is done exclusively at home, there is inevitably a significant number of students who fail to do the work and fall farther and farther behind both in their understanding of the essential concepts of the class and in their ability to pass the class. This is amplified when missing homework receives a zero and homework is a large percentage of the grade. But when teachers use alternatives for finishing student work, like the Ketchup Solution (Reeves, 2012), they can dramatically reduce the failure rate and also have more students engaged on a week-to-week basis. In these creative interventions, students are not absolved from doing their assigned work, but rather must complete it in the "Ketchup" room on Friday mornings. While it certainly would have been better if they had completed the work at home, the vast majority of these students get their work done and enter every weekend with homework complete. When the entire faculty cooperates and shares ownership for the success of all students, teachers save enormous amounts of time in badgering and cajoling students into compliance. Finally, when the definition of *homework* is changed to *practice* and that practice takes place under the guidance of the teacher during the school day, homework compliance dramatically increases, and it also saves the time of teachers who devote hours of evening and weekend time to grading homework and providing feedback that many students do not read. There are many ways faculty may cooperate and share the responsibility for all students' success and change homework into meaningful practice during the school day, including the Friday morning catch-up, the red–yellow–green system, the quiet table, and early finals.

Friday Morning Catch-Up

Students who do not have homework complete report to the Ketchup room and finish their assignments. This typically takes ninety minutes to two hours of Friday morning, and students in regular classes enjoy engaging and fun activities. Nearly every student goes into the weekend with homework complete, and this strategy—with the same students and same faculty—has reduced course failures and discipline problems dramatically (Reeves, 2012).

Red–Yellow–Green System

Nathan Hale High School in Wisconsin pioneered the red–yellow–green system, leaving homework completion between the student and teacher until Thursday afternoon. At that point, teachers classify students into red, yellow, and green groups based on the level of their homework completion and send the counselors the names of students who were classified as yellow or red. Students who had all homework completed were automatically green. Students on the yellow list have a few missing assignments. Students on the red list have many missing assignments and are in danger of failing the class. The counselors compile the results, and the following Monday morning, teachers and paraprofessionals receive the compiled red, yellow, and green lists. These lists are not just the teachers' own students but rather they include students from the entire school. This sends a message that teachers share collective responsibility for every student in the school. This allows teachers in every class, study hall, and even lunch periods to engage in conversations with students like the following.

"You're on the yellow list. I'd like to see your assignment notebook. If you have your work organized and your assignment notebook completed, you're a lot more likely to complete the work. Could you also let me know what kind of help that you need to get back on the green list?"

"You're on the red list, and I really want to help you. Would you please show me your materials for class?"

Requests to see materials for class often result in great resistance from students, but it is a good opportunity for teachers and administrators to determine whether or not students have the essentials for success—pencils, paper, assignment notebooks, textbooks, and so on. If they don't, this provides the opportunity for immediate intervention to get students the support that they need. Moreover, these requests provide a powerful motivation, particularly for adolescent students, to take responsibility for preparing for class and, more important, avoid being on the red list.

Quiet Table

A growing number of schools have started the *quiet table* at lunch, the place where students who do not have homework complete will, with teacher supervision, finish their homework. Lunch periods are usually brief—perhaps twenty to thirty minutes—but that is often enough time to finish missing homework assignments. Most important, the quiet table technique allows peer pressure to be a constructive force. Students love eating together, and when one of their peers is missing from their regular lunch table, one student might say to another, "Come eat with us! Just get your homework done."

There are variations on this strategy in which students who are missing homework eat in a separate room, have restricted study hall privileges, and are otherwise under a greater degree of scrutiny than their peers. The great incentive for many students is freedom from adult supervision and control, and the way to achieve this ideal state is to get homework finished.

Early Finals

In what has been one of the most effective ideas I have ever seen, Ben Davis High School in Indianapolis, a large urban school with more than four thousand students, offers students an early final with the promise that if they earn an A or B on the early final, they have ten days of freedom. Students could not leave campus or wander through the hallways, but they have the ability to choose how to spend those final ten days of class. The students who receive Cs, Ds, or Fs are given specific feedback on the areas that they needed to study for the planned final exam. The results speak for themselves: the passing rate for ninth-grade biology grew from 36 percent the first year, to 69 percent the second year, to 92 percent the third year after the implementation of the early final option. Moreover, the teachers report a striking improvement in morale and efficiency because the last week of school was no longer the chaotic mess it had been when every student had a final exam. From the teachers' perspectives, it was much less stressful to grade and report fifty final exams than one hundred fifty exams. Most important, the exams that teachers graded early resulted in respect for teacher feedback and improved student performance. That resulted in fewer course failures and fewer repeaters in the next semester. Perhaps most significant, the teachers feel that the feedback they provided on the early final was respected—something that they never felt with the traditional final exam.

Reflection

Focusing standards and finding innovative ways to incorporate homework as in-class practice during the school day not only save teachers time but also help to establish and reinforce FAST grading policies that promote learning instead of failure. The following questions will help you and your colleagues identify additional costs of traditional grading policies, take steps to implement improved policies to save teachers time, and focus on benefits that the improved grading policies will bring.

1. Working with your colleagues, think of additional reasons for the teacher time crunch.

2. Consider the time that you spend on proficient versus nonproficient students. What would the time commitment be for teachers who have a higher number of proficient students and a lower number of nonproficient students?

3. What are the time costs for students who fail? Consider not only the costs of remediation but also the costs for disciplinary hearings, suspensions, and expulsions.

4. What is one step that teachers could take to save time? Please focus only on steps that you can control—not anything that requires the approval of the board of education, legislature, superintendent, or even principal—just something that you can do of your own volition.

5. What is one incentive that you could provide for students to take their work more seriously and make a positive commitment to learning? This is not a penalty for failing to meet teacher expectations, but a positive incentive for students to engage in higher levels of learning.

Under time constraints, many teachers struggle with providing feedback to students efficiently, fairly, and effectively. In chapter 6, we'll examine student behavior issues, another challenge to teachers' time, and look at ways to address common behavior problems within the context of a FAST grading system.

Chapter 6

GRADING STUDENT BEHAVIOR

Behavior is an important part of student performance. We expect students to be responsible, respectful, and honest. Too often, debates over grading reform falsely lead observers to conclude that traditional grading practices support personal responsibility and work ethic for students, while grading reform dismisses these qualities. Nothing could be further from the truth. When executed well, grading reform improves student work ethic in a manner that is far more effective than traditional grading practices. The easiest way to test the claim that traditional grading practices are effective is to ask these questions.

- "Is homework compliance at an all-time high?"
- "Is student evidence of personal responsibility and work ethic at an all-time high?"
- "Is cheating at an all-time low?"

If the answers to these questions are in the affirmative, then by all means continue with your practices. But in more than four million miles of travel, I have yet to encounter a school where these statements are true. In fact, I hear frequently that student work ethic is declining, homework compliance is down, and cheating is at an all-time high. If these conclusions are true, then it is not possible to conclude that grading and feedback practices are working to achieve our objectives. These are certainly behaviors that deserve attention but not in the way educators have been dealing with them in the past. Let's consider unexcused absences, tardiness, and academic dishonesty in turn and then reflect on how to improve practices.

Unexcused Absences

Students need to show up to school in order to learn. Or do they? Here is an experiment that you can try in your school. To answer the challenge that teachers should not be accountable for students who fail to attend school, consider how two major metropolitan systems, Milwaukee and Indianapolis, count student performance in two ways. The first measure of performance is the percentage of students who scored proficient or higher on state tests who had attended class 90 percent or more of the time. The second measure is the performance of all students, including those whose attendance was below 90 percent. The districts expected the second measurement to be significantly lower than the first. Sometimes it was, but often it was not. Rather than simply assuming that 90 percent attendance is the minimum required for acceptable student performance, we should at least test that hypothesis.

Many school systems have a rule that if there are ten or more unexcused absences during a semester, then the student automatically fails the class. This rule persists long after educational leaders have rejected seat time as the primary measurement of learning. But old habits are hard to break. Massachusetts is a case in point, particularly during the record-setting winter of 2015 in which the snowfall was the largest ever recorded since the commonwealth began recording the data four hundred years earlier. The Bay State has beautiful spring and fall days, but the winters can be brutal. Even when the streets are plowed, sidewalks remain impassable, and students cannot reach schools or bus stops. This causes an exceptional number of snow days during which schools are closed. Some schools convene on Saturdays to make up the time. Others cancel professional development days. Many go late into June. Some have canceled spring break. This is all based on the premise that students must have seat time in order to learn the content. There is one problem with this policy. Spring tests are delivered on time, whether or not the snow days have been made up. If the seat time hypothesis is true, then tests administered after a hard winter should reflect a steep drop in student performance. That has not been the case. In fact, brutal winters and all, Massachusetts continues to rank among the highest-performing states in the country (Massachusetts Department of Elementary and Secondary Education, 2015). It is therefore disingenuous for state leaders to make speeches that decry seat time and support standards-based learning while at the same time they deny waivers to schools that have irretrievably lost days due to bad weather. In the end, it's all about seat time, not learning.

The rules about unexcused absences also have a host of collateral damages for students and schools. After missing ten days of school, a guaranteed failure provides no incentive for students to attend and, if they do attend, there is no incentive to learn or engage in class activities in any way. A better way to deal with unexcused absences is to provide alternative schedules for students. At Ben Davis High School in Indianapolis, students who have difficulty coming to school during the day have the option to take night classes that allow them to catch up with their peers. Other schools have schedules that allow students and teachers to begin the day at different times, from 7:30 a.m. to after 10:00 a.m. Other schools provide online learning options so that students truly have the opportunity to demonstrate proficiency in a subject, irrespective of the number of hours that they are sitting in class. All of these options are surely better than expelling students after ten days of absence.

Tardiness

Tardiness to class is irritating—in the same way that tardiness to staff meetings, professional learning community (PLC) meetings, and professional development sessions is irritating. There are ways, however, to improve the likelihood that students (and adults) show up on time. Some classes begin precisely on time with essential information, and students who miss that information must remain after class to get it. Some classrooms are arranged so that the front seats (often the least desirable for tardy students) remain open at the beginning of class, so that tardy students must sit in the front. This is also a good strategy for faculty meetings—that is, reserving the front row for those who drift in late to the meeting.

Staff presence in the hallways can also address tardiness. In some schools, every staff member, including teaching and nonteaching staff, is present during passing periods, preventing the shuffling in late to class that often occurs without active adult presence. In other schools, however, passing periods are unattended and dangerous. Bullying, fights, and traffic jams can result in slowing down the schedule for the entire school.

Some penalties for tardiness are counterproductive. For example, when teachers close the door at the sound of the bell and require tardy students to go to the office to get a pass, the student is even later, more likely to interrupt the class, and certainly misses more instruction.

Finally, it is important to consider incentives for prompt attendance rather than penalties for late arrivals. The "points off" threat only registers with students competing for top grades, and they probably arrived early. This has little or no impact on chronically tardy students. Students in general, and adolescents in particular, value choice, power, and competence.

There are ways to integrate choice into every classroom: choice in the projects to build, choice in groups to join, choice in technology tools to use. Choice can be linked to on-time attendance, and constraints on choice are linked to late arrival.

Power is the ability to engage in meaningful assessment—one of the most powerful things that teachers do. Students who engage in accurate self-assessment not only improve their likelihood of success academically but also have a higher degree of motivation due to the self-empowerment that self-assessment provides. Power is a strong motivator to show up on time.

Competence is the third motivator. Consider students who play video games. They keep at it not because of any soft notions of self-esteem; after all, players die at the end of many of these games. Rather, students keep playing again and again because they value the competence that comes with experience. Competence-building exercises can be established not only using technology but also in other forms of interactive classwork. Just as it is the responsibility of teachers to make homework and practice assignments relevant and worth doing, it is also our responsibility to make the early minutes of our class time a space in which choice, power, and competence come alive.

Academic Dishonesty

Cheating is increasing among teenagers in the United States. Eddy Ramírez (2008) reports that:

> 64 percent of high school students surveyed by the Center for Youth Ethics at the Josephson Institute in Los Angeles said they had cheated on a test at least once in the past year, up from 60 percent in 2004. . . . 36 percent said they had used the internet to plagiarize an assignment, up from 33 percent two years ago. . . . 82 percent said they had copied another student's work at least once in the past year. . . . 93 percent of the respondents said that they were satisfied with their personal ethics and character, and 77 percent said that "when it comes to doing what is right, I am better than most people I know."

Although there are sophisticated computer programs that allow teachers to catch obvious examples of cheating, mere replication of a phrase, a sentence, or even a paragraph is not necessarily an indication of cheating. Richard Pérez-Peña (2013) reports on widespread allegations of cheating at Harvard in 2013. In a class of 279, students worked with teaching assistants in the Introduction to Congress course. Students engaged in frequent collaboration and sought the help of graduate students who graded assignments. Pérez-Peña (2013) says:

> Those teaching fellows . . . readily advised students on interpreting exam questions. Administrators said that on final exam questions, some students supplied identical answers, down to, in some cases, typographical errors, indicating that they had written them together or plagiarized them. But some students claimed that the similarities in their answers were due to sharing notes or sitting in on sessions with the same teaching fellows.

Eventually, seventy students were forced to leave the university, and some were eligible to return after a year. Those who chose to fight the allegations faced delays and the university's emotional battering. I don't know if this episode will stop student cheating at Harvard, but I'm pretty sure that it will decrease collaboration among students and teaching fellows. It's just not worth the risk. How should we approach the issues of plagiarism and academic dishonesty?

We must define clearly what academic dishonesty is. I have explained to students at the secondary and collegiate levels that plagiarism is stealing, the same as if I broke into their locker, car, or home and took things. For a writer like me, words are my property, and stealing them is a crime. Many students are shocked at the analogy, because stealing words to them is like stealing music off the web—their parents do it, and everyone they know does it, too. The rock stars they see are all doing well financially, so they think of themselves as 21st century Robin Hoods, stealing from the rich to give to the poor. It doesn't help that their parents are stealing property from the Internet. Some others in positions of authority, such as church choir directors, regularly use photocopied music rather than paying the publisher and composer for original copies. When teachers and professors distribute illegally copied articles or book chapters, it's difficult to understand their righteous indignation at the offenses of their students. Students, therefore, need a clear definition of what conduct is honest and what is dishonest, and then teachers and administrators must pledge to adhere to the same code of conduct.

Second, we should consider carefully the appropriate consequences for academic dishonesty. If students vandalized a fence, we could expel them from school or, more constructively, have them repair the fence and perhaps perform other community service. If students stole an electronic device, we could expel them from school, or we could have them not only replace the device but also engage in penance that is meaningful and time consuming, not something that their parents can buy but something that the students must do. And if students cheated and plagiarized, we could expel them, or we could require that they complete the assignment—perhaps more than one—honestly. The key is that many students arrive in school simply not understanding what academic dishonesty means, and someone has to tell them.

Third, we must explain what academic dishonesty is not. Collaborating with peers, providing meaningful feedback on their work, and expecting the same from fellow students is not cheating. Most people will work in teams throughout their entire careers, and most school districts give rhetorical flourishes in their mission and vision statements to 21st century skills, including collaboration. If we believe in the value of collaboration and teamwork, then we should expect students to produce common work products.

FAST Feedback for Behavior

Student behavior matters, and it matters so much that we should not conflate behavior with academic performance. Primary teachers get this right. One part of the report card covers student literacy and mathematics skills, while another part of the report card addresses student ability to play well with others, follow directions, and behave in class. But after the primary grades, reflections of student behavior become part of academic grades, and the grades lose their credibility as an accurate indicator of student performance.

If we want to improve behavior, then feedback on absences, tardiness, dishonesty, and other behaviors that we wish to discourage must receive the same FAST feedback that we provide in the academic arena. That is, behavioral feedback must be fair, accurate, specific, and timely. Fairness requires that students with similar offenses be treated in a similar manner. Fairness is about consistency in the application of consequences.

FAST feedback for behavior also requires accuracy. As the Harvard example indicates, the mere appearance of similar work could be a result of cheating, and it could also be the result of getting the same answer to the same question from a graduate teaching assistant (Pérez-Peña, 2013). In large lecture classes where students are expected to demonstrate proficiency by regurgitating the content from the professor's lecture, we should not be surprised that many students, equipped with computers and recording devices, will parrot precisely what the professor said. If the professors and teachers really wanted original work, they would not ask for answers based on content but for a synthesis and evaluation of course content that would necessarily be different for each student. As a graduate student, I regularly participated in study groups with four other students, particularly in difficult courses such as statistics. The five of us worked together to better understand the course. I'm sure that our answers to assignments were remarkably similar. As an advisor to graduate students, I also encourage collaborative work, including the sharing of citations, literature reviews, and research methods. It has never occurred to me that any of these collaborative efforts would be regarded as cheating, but a meat-ax approach that disregards the fundamental principles of fairness and accuracy will certainly destroy these sorts of collaborative efforts.

FAST feedback on behavior also requires specificity. If we wish to change student behavior—and that is a large part of what school is all about—then we need to be clear about conduct that is acceptable and unacceptable. We need to make the expectations we have for students clear. When they violate those expectations, we should be similarly clear about the precise nature of their offense and how they can improve their conduct in the future.

Finally, feedback on behavior must be timely. As soon as students commit an offense, educators must confront them, and they must change the behavior. Tardy students remain after class. Absent students have a consequence that is not failure, but rather a consequence that entails a different learning environment and the opportunity to show proficiency. When students cheat, it should not require a lengthy investigation but a clear presentation of the evidence and an immediate opportunity for the student to respond to it. The most effective consequence is learning the precise nature of the offense and making amends by doing the assignment honestly.

The point of this chapter is not to suggest that students are always right or that bad behavior should be acceptable. Rather, educators should expect that students arrive to schools not fully formed, and it is their job at every level of education to teach students about behavior as well as about academic content. Educators will not always succeed the first time. But if educators expect behavior to improve, they must focus on the behavior by calling it what it is and not confusing it with academic content.

Reflection

Reflect on your responses to student behavior issues, including unexcused absences, tardiness, and academic dishonesty. Use the exercises below to examine areas where you might improve the fairness, accuracy, specificity, and timeliness of the responses to and consequences for students' misbehavior.

1. Think of students you have encountered with large numbers of unexcused absences. In figure 6.1, record your consequences for those students. What would you consider as alternative consequences that would increase the likelihood of student success?

Current Consequences for Absences	Alternative Consequences for Absences

Figure 6.1: Considering consequences for student absences.

*Visit **go.solution-tree.com/assessment** for a free reproducible version of this figure.*

2. In figure 6.2, review your consequences for tardiness. What alternative consequences could you consider?

Current Consequences for Tardiness	Alternative Consequences for Tardiness

Figure 6.2: Considering consequences for tardiness.

*Visit **go.solution-tree.com/assessment** for a free reproducible version of this figure.*

3. In figure 6.3, consider what your consequences for academic dishonesty are now and how they might be revised to better achieve the goal of students who behave ethically in all matters.

Current Consequences for Academic Dishonesty	Alternative Consequences for Academic Dishonesty

Figure 6.3: Considering consequences for academic dishonesty.

*Visit **go.solution-tree.com/assessment** for a free reproducible version of this figure.*

A FAST approach to feedback can help educators ensure that their responses to student behavior outline effective consequences and promote learning from the offense and making amends. In chapter 7, we turn our attention to the lessons educators can learn from FAST feedback practices in physical education and the arts and how they can incorporate those practices into their own classrooms.

Part III

Considering FAST Feedback Throughout Schools, Systems, and Communities

Chapter 7

LEARNING FROM PHYSICAL EDUCATION AND THE ARTS

Craig Ross is the chief executive officer (CEO) of Verus Global, an international provider of corporate training programs. The organization has experienced dramatic growth under his leadership (C. Ross, personal communication, March 15, 2015). The author of several books, he is also a dynamic presenter and leader. But when I first met Craig, he was the basketball coach at a small college and a student in one of my graduate school classes. He was a gifted student, and I often wondered how he had time to balance all of his responsibilities. He was particularly animated when he talked about effective feedback and deliberate practice, because these were ideas that he lived by in his role as a coach. After I watched him in action, I incorporated an observation of his practice and work during games into my graduate school assessment class.

Whenever I address the value of athletics and the arts as models for effective feedback, eyes inevitably roll. Either people don't see any connection to these activities and academic pursuits, or they are certain that these activities have little relationship to their individual environment. Uncooperative kids can be cut from the football team or dismissed from the marching band, but we have to deal with the students we have, they say. That may be true for professional teams and major college activities, but in a small liberal arts school, the coaches and music teachers labor under the same conditions as class-room teachers. Certainly, in the bands and choruses of elementary, middle, and high schools, the same students come to every other class in the school.

Craig's team was similar to this. He had no recruiting budget, no scholarships, and no enticements to offer players except for the love of the game. Yet, he was remarkably successful as a coach. I asked my students to watch his practices, noting the nature of feedback that he provided to the players and how the players responded to it. A couple of things stood out. First, every player on the team, including those on the bench, received a steady dose of feedback. Second, the coach focused on a single improvement—not a speech with four things to do. Third, other players leveraged feedback. Students on the court reinforced what the coach said on the sidelines. Fourth, and most important, observers could see the result of the feedback within minutes—even seconds—as the players adjusted their play based on the team's needs and coach's feedback.

This experience changed the way that I teach. For each assignment, I created clear rubrics and made every effort to grade student assignments immediately, sometimes while on a break during a three-hour seminar, so that students could receive same-day feedback. I broke down my feedback into small and manageable segments so that students knew exactly how to improve for their next draft. I also required students to attach a self-assessment using the same rubric that I would use as they turned in the assignment. I expected them to engage not only in self-assessment but in peer assessment before the assignment was submitted to me. Most important, I was able to check the value of my feedback based on the student responses to it. Often, I hear teachers complain that the second draft of an assignment contains the same errors, only with neater handwriting. When students don't know what the teacher wants, they have little choice but to default to what they can do. But when we provide clear and explicit feedback as Craig did for his team, we can reasonably expect students to act on it.

This chapter includes some of the most important lessons we can learn from our colleagues in the arts and athletics: lessons from failure, response to feedback, peer support for learning, and critical thinking. Too often, we place these objectives in the hands of advocates of 21st century skills who dominate YouTube videos. That may be entertaining, but the path to these learning opportunities is right outside your door and down the hallway leading to the music room and gymnasium.

Lessons From Failure

Many readers recall the Broadway musical *The Music Man* in which Harold Hill, the salesman turned band director, seduced the entire town of River City, Iowa, with his notion that a band would solve the problems of delinquency among the city's pool-playing boys (DaCosta, 1962). Equipped with uniforms and band instruments, the students in *The Music Man* were able, in the final scenes, to offer a painful rendition of the "Minuet in G" with clarinets squeaking and more wrong notes than right ones. But in a flash, the band breaks out into the famous "Seventy-Six Trombones" that I hope you will hum for the rest of the week. This transformation was instantaneous only in the world of Broadway shows and movies. But music teachers see it every year, encouraging students to progress from painful productions at the beginning of the semester to performances at which parents, teachers, and fellow students justifiably applaud. Coaches take students who barely understand the rules of the game, have never seen a playbook, and have more enthusiasm than talent and mold them into a competitive team.

Pat Summitt coached the University of Tennessee women's basketball team to more than one thousand wins while maintaining a 100 percent graduation rate, a feat unequaled in college sports (Pat Summitt Foundation, n.d.). Summitt focused on the fundamentals, even though she recruited players who believed they already had mastered the fundamentals. University of California, Los Angeles (UCLA) Coach John Wooden won ten national championships in a twelve-year period. But when he was asked what he did for a living, he emphatically replied that he was a teacher. Although students with enormous talent came to his team, he began each year the same way—by teaching students how to put on their socks and shoes. They practiced it again and again until they got it just right. Wooden's practices were meticulously planned in extensive handwritten notes on pages of legal pads, and he spent more time planning a practice than the practice took. But as good as Summitt's and Wooden's players were, they were the athletic equivalent of Harold Hill's band at the beginning of every year. It took time, practice, and enormous quantities of feedback to transform a group of individual players into national championship teams.

Can you imagine Pat Summitt, John Wooden, or the most successful music teachers that you know averaging the results of the first days of the semester in with the final days? Can you imagine them awarding zeroes for failure? These educators expect failure and use each failure as an opportunity to improve student performance and their own teaching strategies. Wooden rewrote his lesson plans—that is, his practice plans—every day based on his observations the previous day. He provided individual, small-group, and whole-group instruction.

I have observed the same practice techniques by observing some of the great symphony and choral conductors of our age: James Levine, formerly with the Boston Symphony Orchestra and now with the Metropolitan Opera; Scott Jarrett of the Back Bay Chorale, Charlotte Symphony, and Marsh Chapel Collegium; and Rafael Frühbeck de Burgos, who, in his eighties, manages a global conducting career of the classical and new music repertoire. These conductors are dealing with professional musicians. How could they possibly fail? It turns out that they fail frequently. The difference between the beginning of the rehearsal and the end of it is astonishing. The Boston Symphony Orchestra, the Back Bay Chorale, and the Marsh Chapel Collegium attract some of the best musicians throughout the world, yet they still learn from failure during every practice. What is particularly worthy of notice is that none of these professional musicians seem offended when the conductor asks them to reconsider how they are playing, and then do it again, and again, and again, and again. This is why students at every level need a coach who will help them engage in deliberative practice. Great coaches identify the most challenging passages—not just in music, but in reading, writing, science, social studies, art, physical education, and every other endeavor. Failure is the path to success, and I've never seen great conductors grade a rehearsal; I've only seen them seek to improve the performance of the players they are leading.

Response to Feedback

Compare the response to feedback from an exceptionally hardworking English teacher to that from an equally hardworking coach. My college composition teacher, Professor Hillier, was an extraordinary Shakespeare scholar. He would read poetry to our class that would make him weep, and in so doing he brought the entire class into his world of concise expression, precise words, and expressive writing. But his greatest gifts to students were the paragraph-long comments that he made on our weekly essays. Although he had been honing his teaching skills since World War II, he never got faster at the task of giving students feedback; he only got better. Although he gave us the opportunity to apply his feedback for improved writing, only a few students took him up on his offer. The scores of hours that he spent providing feedback to students was wasted on the young.

Contrast the efforts of the beloved Professor Hillier with his colleagues in music, art, drama, and athletics. I watched the same students emerge from Professor Hillier's class go to the nearby theater and, following the feedback from the music director, improve their every movement, every word, every note. I was equally guilty of this, as I would leave the composition class without changing a syllable of an essay, and go to a music lesson in which I labored over every measure, responding to feedback immediately and improving the quality of my work. It was not until Professor Hillier announced that his honors students were failing his class that we finally realized that his labors at giving us feedback required respect. The same students in classes for arts and athletics were used to receiving feedback and responding immediately.

We know that feedback is one of the most powerful influences on student achievement, but as these vignettes illustrate, merely the provision of feedback is not enough. The most well-intentioned teachers can provide feedback that meets all of the FAST criteria, but if students do not understand and apply the feedback, then teachers and students squander these sincere efforts at feedback. The lesson from the arts and athletics is that feedback has an influence only if there is an immediate, and sometimes dramatic, impact on the student. Consider the young artist Monet, who was immensely frustrated at traditional judges' rejection of his work at the Paris Exposition in the middle of the 19th century. Monet and his colleagues sought alternative sources of feedback and established their own exhibition, at great risk, and decided to let viewers decide the merits of their work. The result of that alternative exhibition now forms the genesis of the impressionist movement. A century earlier, the young musician Wolfgang Amadeus Mozart was criticized by his patron, the emperor, who reportedly said, "too many notes, Herr Mozart, too many notes" (Elson, 1909, pp. 235–236). Johann Sebastian Bach's music met with similar criticism decades earlier. Half of his cantatas are lost to posterity because local butchers used the musical manuscripts to wrap meat. But Bach moved from one church to another until he found the essential compatibility between the provision of feedback and the application of it to create wonderful works of music. Despite his early setbacks, Bach's work nevertheless influenced generations of musicians and continues in the 21st century to dominate the chromatic structure of classical and contemporary music.

Bach died in 1750, Mozart died in 1791, and Monet and Hillier have joined them in the great beyond. Yet, their lessons on response to feedback remain deeply relevant in the 21st century. Specifically, they teach us that precision in feedback is insufficient if it does not influence the result. Without a team, John Wooden and Pat Summitt would just be more voices in the wilderness. These great teachers knew that they not only provided feedback but also created a great feedback environment in which students had multiple sources of feedback and the opportunity to make immediate improvements. Wooden and Summitt constructed practices in ways that provided students with feedback not only from the coaches but from fellow students. Monet received feedback from more than the judges of the Paris Exposition, but from other sources, including the public who saw more in his initial impressionist works than the official judges saw. FAST feedback, in brief, requires not only the fundamentals of fairness, accuracy, specificity, and timeliness but also a delivery system that provides multiple channels of feedback for students.

Peer Support for Learning

Even in small schools, the music teacher often has the largest student-to-teacher ratio in the entire school. Coaches typically have many more students in practice than teachers might have in their algebra or history classes. How do they manage? Almost all of them have a tradition of student leadership in which experienced students take on the role of peer leader, providing feedback, support, and encouragement to other players. The same is true in the most successful professional learning communities, where students have a variety of support systems, including not only teachers but also their fellow students. Many elementary schools, including the Advent School in Boston, have a reading buddies program in which fifth- and sixth-grade students coach children in early childhood centers, kindergarten, and first grade so that the younger students develop the same joy in reading that their older reading buddies have enjoyed. The students dress as characters of the stories they most enjoy and immerse themselves in the details of characters, plot, and setting. Similarly, students in Suzuki music classes will, with eighty students on a stage, take their cues not only from the conductor but also from one another. In athletic practices too large and complicated for a single coach to support every player, careful attention to the dialogue among players quickly reveals another situation in which students receive feedback not only from the coach but also from fellow students.

This only works, however, if coaches, conductors, and teachers clearly communicate their expectations for performance and skills to their teams and students. For example, if the Suzuki conductor expects *forte*, a louder sound, and the peer coach expects *piano*, a softer sound, then the feedback system will be imprecise and confusing. But when the teachers at the helm are clear about their expectations, then every move, whether of fingers on the violin or feet on the basketball court, becomes orchestrated.

There are three keys for effective peer support for learning that programs like reading buddies exhibit. First, the peer coach must be a master of the discipline. Note that mastery is not superiority. It's entirely possible that the seventh-grade violinist or basketball player is superior to the eighth-grade coach. But the eighth-grade coach must know the discipline with sufficient depth to distinguish among different levels of performance.

Second, the peer coach must be capable of honest and empathetic feedback. "That's wrong!" is unspecific feedback that can be a temptation for the peer coach, so students must be led to understand what effective feedback looks like. Too often we look at the result rather than causes. Great coaches focus on the causes. Yelling "You missed the basket!" or "That was a wrong note!" are not nearly as effective as quiet discussions of foot placement and arm movement in basketball and finger placement in music. Great coaches, including peer coaches, think several steps ahead of the wrong moves. Before a layup in basketball is the placement of the student's feet on the court. Before the pianist's fingers hit the keys is the position of the piano bench. And as John Wooden patiently explained for half a century, before you walk onto the floor, your socks and shoes have to be put on correctly.

Third, peer coaches must focus on performance, not talk. We all tend to teach in the way in which we were taught. This perhaps explains the continued use of 14th century lectures in the 21st century. But like other vestigial parts of our genealogical inheritance, lectures will eventually diminish. Early in my career, I thought a good lecture consisted of ruffles and flourishes, planned meticulously from the first to the ninetieth minute. Today, I know that effective presentations involve interaction from the first moment, including texts, emails, tweets, and whatever the next communication innovation will be. The ninetieth minute is unknown, because the dialogue with the audience, both those physically present and those engaging with me from around the world, will be far more important than my meticulous plans. Audiences in staff development presentations have the experience and insight that I lack, and I had better listen to them. Peer insights, even on the stage in front of a thousand people, are as vital as they are for reading buddies.

Critical Thinking

Regardless of whether a teacher, coach, or peer provides feedback, observations must be grounded in and must encourage critical thinking for students to derive maximum benefit. The essence of critical thinking is to compare a claim against the evidence. It's difficult to imagine the prototypical, imperious, and demanding coach or music conductor valuing critical thinking. As the old cartoon character, Quick Draw McGraw, used to say, "I'll do the thinnin' around here!" But that's not what I observed among the best athletic and musical leaders.

As I watched the Boston Symphony Orchestra rehearse, I noticed that Maestro James Levine would ask not the concertmaster but a musician deep into the stands to take the baton and listen to a particular passage. He would ask another musician to put down her instrument and go to the back of Symphony Hall and listen critically to the orchestra and provide feedback to the maestro. Amateur coaches and bandleaders yell at their students in the same way that amateur fans yell at their televisions in equally futile attempts to influence the action. The best coaches and musical directors I have studied never raised their voices. They certainly did not raise their voices against students who were critical thinkers. When Levine would hand the baton, the power sword of the musical world, to the fourth violist, he was interested in listening to alternatives, to different interpretations of the music. Critical thinking is not about criticism, but rather about comparing one's previous convictions to the available alternatives. I have in my collection a dozen versions of Beethoven's Ninth Symphony, and my sixth-grade daughter wanders about the apartment singing "Alle Menschen werden Brüder"—the famous words of the poet Johann Christoph Friedrich von Schiller, "All mankind shall be brothers" (Hamerman, 1993). Each version is different in tempo, style, and emphasis, but they all follow Beethoven's manuscript.

Critical thinking requires a comparison of the claim—the historical context of the work—to the evidence of information available to us. In sports, for example, football has evolved over the years, and depending on one's viewpoint, the forward pass would not be part of the game had it not been for Harvard—or perhaps Yale.

Billie Jean King transformed the world of women's tennis with her aggressive play that defeated her male opponent, Bobby Riggs. Critical thinking requires challenging accepted conventions, and each of these examples does that.

While critical thinking is part of the canon of 21st century skills, it is honored more in the breach than the observance. If the challenge to common assumptions is to be honored, then teachers who, for example, challenge the prevailing orthodoxy of tests as a measure of teacher evaluation should be celebrated rather than ostracized. A teacher who challenges value-added evaluation systems should be given a fair hearing rather than denounced as someone who has insufficient buy-in. Administrators who challenge the artificial ratings of schools on an A to F scale should be recognized as thinkers rather than oppositional figures of the old school who just don't get it. To be fair, people on the other side of these debates also deserve a fair hearing and due respect. One of the great tragedies of our era is the failure of respectful policy debates. Challenges to character, personal motivation, and professional intent prevail over the clash of opposing ideas.

Reflection

If there is a singular message from this chapter, it is that there are frequently colleagues very close to us who offer keys to effective feedback. Even if they don't provide letter grades, they can provide FAST feedback, and their work provides fair, accurate, specific, and timely feedback to students and to themselves. This could be a model for the entire school. Consider the following questions to start the conversation about how educators in your school respond to failure, elicit the greatest response from students to feedback, support learning from peers, and encourage and discourage critical thinking.

1. In figure 7.1, reflect on the response to failure in your school. How might you reconsider failure for students, teachers, and administrators?

	Current Response to Failure	Alternative Response to Failure
Students		
Teachers		
Administrators		

Figure 7.1: Considering responses to failure.

*Visit **go.solution-tree.com/assessment** for a free reproducible version of this figure.*

2. How could you elicit the greatest response from students to the feedback that teachers provide? Consider not only the feedback provided but also the multiple channels of feedback.

3. In figure 7.2, consider how peer support for learning occurs in your school. How could it be improved based on the examples in this chapter?

Current Peer Support Systems	Alternative Peer Support Systems

Figure 7.2: Considering peer support for learning.

*Visit **go.solution-tree.com/assessment** for a free reproducible version of this figure.*

4. Consider the ways in which your system promotes and discourages critical thinking. How could teachers learn from their colleagues in music and athletics about critical thinking?

Feedback practices from physical education, music, and the arts can strengthen FAST grading practices in the classroom. We can learn valuable strategies from colleagues outside our own classrooms. The case study in chapter 8 illustrates how communicating with colleagues across a school district and within the community can deepen best practices for teaching, leadership, and grading.

Chapter 8

CONSIDERING THE CONTEXTS OF TEACHING AND LEADING

In this final chapter, we consider the essentials of reflective practice on grading alongside best practices for teaching and leading. This book has made the claim that effective grading practices are not merely the province of the classroom teacher but rather must be the subject of a collaborative enterprise within the school and throughout the system. Moreover, effective grading requires the support of governing board policies and community leaders.

This chapter presents the experiences of a newly consolidated district and demonstrates how communicating openly, identifying challenges to best practices, and discussing school system expectations and community realities can support grading practices within a larger context of teaching and leading. As schools make the transition toward improved grading and more effective instructional and leadership practices, it is essential that teachers break free from their disciplinary silos. They must also break free from silos associated with grade levels and community history and culture.

Communicating Openly

Unified School District 23 is a small system in a rural area of the Midwest. It was created because the population had steadily declined and the four communities within the district could no longer sustain having their own K–12 systems. Even though the district bore the label *unified*, it was anything but unified. Moving from four school boards and four superintendents to one had been challenging for these close-knit communities. The new superintendent, Alma Nielsen, was an outsider from a neighboring community about an hour's drive away. She learned quickly that one of her primary jobs was to soothe the almost constant feelings among the community leaders of the four towns in the district that their interests were not being considered. Everything from the bus routes and the cafeteria food to the schedule for board meetings was perceived as a slight to one community or another. Moreover, the board members who hired her were often focused on representing their community constituents more than the school system as a whole. She convened a meeting of the four communities' faculty leaders with the request that they combine their best thinking about effective teaching practices. Her intent was to be relentlessly positive and bring a spirit of teamwork to the combined K–12 system. This meeting, she hoped, would begin the foundation of creating a professional learning community within District 23.

She began the meeting by saying, "I really appreciate that the four of you took time to meet with me. My goal for the meeting is to have us engage in a collegial conversation about teaching and learning. I know that you're doing great work, and I'd specifically like to learn about the best practices you have observed among your colleagues. I'd also like us to engage in critical thinking. By that, I mean not offering personal criticism, but rather considering the degree to which the evidence available to us supports our conclusions. If you ask a colleague for evidence, that's not a personal challenge, but a professional inquiry. In fact, we won't get better if we don't seek evidence to support our conclusions. I'm confident that the four of you can lead the way for our entire K–12 faculty in this process. Mr. French, let's begin with you."

Freeman French was a music teacher whose work included K–12 responsibilities. He was one of the longest-serving teachers in the district. His days were busy doing everything from teaching choral music in the primary grades to conducting the middle and high school bands. Few students had access to private music lessons, so much of Mr. French's weekend and after-school time was devoted to helping students learn the basics of their instruments. He was known for his strict demeanor but also his nearly constant attention to students' individual needs. Although his classes were electives at the middle and high school levels, he always had full enrollment, and even students who were not taking his classes often sought his advice on dealing with conflict and preparing for life after high school.

Superintendent Nielsen began the conversation by asking Mr. French to reflect on the best teaching practices he had seen from his K–12 perspective. Mr. French said, "It's been a difficult transition trying to bring four communities together, but I think the music program represents something that everyone supports. We have had great attendance at our concerts, and during football games everyone seems to appreciate our halftime performances. Even though we are in Division 1-A, the smallest in the state, our band almost always has more students than the schools we play against. I've also seen some great work by our coaches, who have been really cooperative with me. We have students who quickly trade their football uniforms for their band uniforms and hustle onto the field to join the band at halftime. You never see that in larger schools. I've also seen some really strong work in student writing at almost every level. When I ask students to reflect on their performances, as I do every Monday, their paragraphs are well organized and thoughtful. That's a great reflection on our elementary teachers as well as the English language arts faculty in the middle and high schools."

"That's a great way to start our meeting," said Ms. Nielsen. "Could you also suggest some improvements that we might make?"

Mr. French hesitated, and then said, "I wish that I could collaborate more closely with our mathematics teachers. When I talk with students about musical concepts, like thirds and fifths, they give me blank stares. These are notions that they should have learned in elementary school, but even my middle and high school students have trouble with it. I have similar problems explaining things like 4/4 time—four beats to a measure and a quarter note getting one beat. It's even difficult for them to understand that two eighth notes have the same value as one quarter note. I don't mean this as any criticism, because I know that our mathematics faculty work incredibly hard, but I hope that we might consider better collaboration, perhaps with including some musical examples in their classes. In fact, I'd be willing to spend some time during my planning period to do a mathematics lesson on these concepts."

Dr. Alan Moore, the chairman of the mathematics department, jumped in. "Thanks, Freeman," he began, "but we have already got a full plate. As I'm sure you've noticed, our mathematics scores are terrible, and one reason is exactly what you said—that our students don't even know basic fractions. How can we teach them algebra and geometry when they don't know basic number operations?"

"Please wait a moment," said Ms. Nielsen. "You'll have your chance to speak in a moment."

Dr. Moore was not used to waiting to speak. He was used to being the most authoritative person in the room, and he had been a finalist for the superintendent's position. Although he respected Ms. Nielsen, he could not help but believe that he could do a better job at almost everything she was attempting.

"Ms. Gunzelman, I believe you're next," said Ms. Nielsen. "Please tell us about the best practices you have observed and how we might improve."

Identifying Challenges to Best Practices

Ernestine Gunzelman was a fifth-grade teacher known for her long lectures (at least in the eyes of fifth graders) about everything from citizenship and discipline to history. She was a master of the fifth-grade curriculum and knew that her most important task was to get students ready for the rigors of middle school. Her lesson plans were meticulously prepared, and other teachers often sought her advice on both the content of the curriculum and classroom management.

She replied directly to Ms. Nielsen, saying, "I really want to support my colleagues, but I must say that our newer teachers really don't know their subjects very well. When the consolidation happened, we lost several teachers, and our new teachers are clearly not going to stay here. For many of them, going to a small rural district was just a way to get a job before they move back to the city. I don't mind giving them advice, but it's just exhausting because they come here not knowing the state standards, not knowing how to create curriculum and assessments, and not knowing how to discipline their students."

"OK," said the superintendent. "Could you tell us about best practices among your colleagues that might benefit the entire district?"

"Sure," replied Ms. Gunzelman. "I agree with Freeman that our coaches do a great job. They work across the grade levels and really help our elementary students to learn discipline and follow directions. Our primary teachers are also pretty good, and a lot of their students are reading on grade level by the end of second grade. It's been hard for them, though, because we've had an influx of immigrants whose parents work at the chicken-processing plant. They tend to be quiet and well behaved, but they are really struggling to learn English when their parents only speak Spanish at home."

"Could I just ask a favor?" Ms. Nielsen interrupted. "Many of the students of parents who moved here from Mexico and Central America were born in the United States. They're not immigrants; they are U.S. citizens. I'd really like us to regard them as part of our community, even if they are still learning English. Ms. Gunzelman, is there anything else you'd like to share?" she continued.

"Thank you, Ms. Nielsen. It is important for our students to feel like they are a part of the community," Ms. Gunzelman responded. "Considering all of my students, I've got to say that my class leads the way and sets the standard for the school. I think I'm the only teacher who covers the complete curriculum, and I almost never send students to the principal's office. My students know what I expect, and they know that there are consequences for not finishing homework, speaking out of turn, or doing badly on a test. My job is to get them ready for middle school, and I think I do that pretty well," she continued.

"All right," said the superintendent. "Let's hear from Mr. Wingo."

Wayne Wingo was the middle school social studies teacher and also an assistant football coach for the high school. He was a history major and wanted to go to graduate school. But with money tight and student loans to pay, he enrolled in a thirteen-month program to get his master's in curriculum and instruction and got a teaching license. He was in his fifth year at the middle school and was attempting to settle into the community. He was quickly recognized for his historical knowledge and also took time to learn the other parts of the social studies curriculum for sixth, seventh, and eighth grades, teaching geography, economics, U.S. history, and world history. People also appreciated that he was becoming a volunteer historian for the four towns in the district, and that made the town leaders feel respected and appreciated.

"Middle school is tough," began Mr. Wingo. "I really appreciate and respect all that Ms. Gunzelman had to say, but between raging hormones and the increasing demands for rigor in our curriculum, it's just really difficult to feel adequately prepared. Also, because English and mathematics are emphasized most on the state test, students are constantly being pulled out of my class to learn the basics. They don't have a chance on my tests because they weren't in class to learn the material."

"I understand," said Ms. Nielsen. "But I'm really trying to learn about best teaching practices in the middle school."

"Well," began Mr. Wingo, "our English teachers do pretty well, considering the challenges that they face. I heard somewhere that it takes kids five to seven years to learn a new language, so even our English learners who have been here for several years really don't know English very well. While I'm not happy about them being pulled out of my class, I do respect how hard the English teachers are working to try to get these students up to speed. Of course, Mr. French does a great job in music. I can't believe how excited students are to go to his class, even when they either slept or were inattentive in my class. I can't make them listen or take notes, but I can ensure that I address the curriculum. I think they like learning about history, but some find it pretty boring. And even though our English teachers are doing a great job, a lot of students still struggle with reading the textbook. I've been trying to have them read some historical documents to get them ready for high school, but they really zone out when they can't comprehend what they're reading. And the charts and graphs in the economics curriculum? Forget about it! They just don't know how to read them, interpret them, or create them."

"We understand, Mr. Wingo," said the superintendent. "But aren't there some best practices at the middle school that we can learn from?"

"Wayne is right on," interrupted Dr. Moore. "They don't know the basics of charts and graphs, either."

"You'll have your chance in a minute," said Ms. Nielsen. "Mr. Wingo, please give us some best practices that we can learn from."

"The new art teacher is really great, even though she's only part-time. You've probably seen the displays of student artwork around the building. It really perks people up, and the kids leave it alone. It's the first time since I've been here that student work has been displayed like this. And she labels the artwork with words in English and Spanish so that students can better understand the words. And the art class is the one place where our English learners seem to shine," Mr. Wingo replied.

"Thanks," said Ms. Nielsen. "Dr. Moore, please tell us about best practices in the high school," she requested.

Discussing System and Community Expectations and Realities

"Well, I'm not going to pull any punches. We all know that fewer than half of our kids go to college, community college, or technical school. Even the kids who go usually don't graduate," Dr. Moore began. "I know of only a few students who have completed four-year degrees after they leave here. They almost all say that they want to move out of here, but they wind up working in the chicken plant or on their parents' farms, but most of those family farms are being bought by corporate farms, so there just isn't much for them to look forward to."

"I understand," said Ms. Nielsen, "but I'm asking for best practices in the high school."

"Right," said Dr. Moore. "I agree with Wayne Wingo that Freeman French does a great job in music. And I wish our social studies teacher knew her content as well as Mr. Wingo does. I think I do a good job teaching mathematics, even though our test scores don't reflect it. We're required to teach algebra, geometry, and trigonometry to every student, even though the vast majority of them are just not ready for it. I've got a lot of seniors in classes designed for freshmen because they have flunked the same mathematics class more than once. These kids are really frustrated, because even though they love art and music, they just can't fit it into their schedule. And let's not forget the elephant in the room. We had eighty students enter ninth grade, but our senior class has fewer than fifty students. I guess that's better than some other rural districts, but it's really discouraging for me to conform to state mathematics requirements when I feel that I'm just driving kids away from school. Okay, so you really want me to talk about best practices? Our principal and counselor do a really great job creating an orderly environment. The three biggest troublemakers last year were expelled, the hallways are quiet and safe, and we didn't have a single incident of alcohol on school grounds this year. That's a big improvement from the previous few years. I think that our vocational teacher has created a wonderful program in collaboration with the technical school, and he's trying very hard to prepare students for real jobs. He even does mock job interviews with them so that they can apply for part-time jobs while they are going to school and full-time jobs after they leave. He's also cooperated with some local farmers to have the kids learn to work on farm machinery like combines and tractors—skills that the kids can really use in many places around the region."

Dr. Moore wanted to expand on his concerns about academic disciplines. He knew that the middle school teachers meant well, but the ninth-grade class was just not ready for high school. He thought that Ms. Nielsen's expectations for students were not realistic. It was clear at the beginning of ninth grade who was going to college and who wasn't, and Dr. Moore was still dealing with parents who were resentful of the consolidation of the four communities into one district.

Reflection

Although grading policies can be the source of deep divisions within schools and communities, the values surrounding effective grading policies can bring faculty, governing board members, and community leaders together. While there are often divisions about educational policies, there can be common ground on the values of fairness, accuracy, specificity, and timeliness. Advocates of the mathematics team and football team, cheerleading squad and debate squad, philosophy club and spelling club, Future Farmers, and Future Teachers can all agree on these fundamental values. With your team, use the following questions to guide your reflection on what you might learn about grading, teaching, and leadership practices from individuals within the school as well as throughout the educational system, governing board, and community.

1. Return to the text of the conversation and underline or highlight each conclusion that the participants have made. Now put yourself in the position of Ms. Nielsen, the superintendent. What questions could you ask of this group to get the teachers to engage in more critical thinking? Ms. Nielsen described critical thinking as professional inquiry about the degree to which available evidence supports our conclusions. Think about the conclusions that the participants in the meeting have drawn, and then pose questions to elicit evidence about those conclusions in figure 8.1.

Conclusions	Requests for Evidence

Figure 8.1: Asking for evidence to support conclusions.

*Visit **go.solution-tree.com/assessment** for a free reproducible version of this figure.*

2. Based on this discussion, what are the primary success stories in this district? What are some additional success stories that, with enough inquiry, you might uncover with additional questions?

3. What are the most important challenges the district is facing?

4. What specific strategies would you recommend for the district? Use figure 8.2 to consider strategies in professional learning, feedback to students, observation and evaluation of teachers, and other strategies that you would recommend.

Focus Area	Instructional and Leadership Strategies
Professional Learning	
Feedback to Students	
Observation and Evaluation	
Other Instructional and Leadership Strategies	

Figure 8.2: Instructional and leadership strategies to support focus areas.

Visit **go.solution-tree.com/assessment** *for a free reproducible version of this figure.*

FAST grading is neither quick nor simple, but the rewards can be exceptional. Although the evidence in this book comes from around the world, you don't have to look very far to find examples of feedback that is fair, accurate, specific, and timely. On the athletic field, in the music room, in the theater, and many other areas throughout the school, teachers provide feedback that meets all of these criteria. The most casual observer can notice how students respond to the feedback and how their performance improves. These minute-to-minute improvements in student results yield tremendous dividends, including reduced failure rates, better discipline, and improved faculty morale. If our colleagues in music, athletics, and theater are not present during your next discussion of grading policies, you might want to invite them.

Discussions about improving grading practices have sometimes become unnecessarily toxic, filled with misunderstandings and anger. But as the examples in these pages suggest, it is possible to have thoughtful and positive discussions about grading and, more broadly, effective teaching and learning. Productive discussions respect the professional judgment of classroom teachers and engage every stakeholder, including parents and students. We can assure even the most skeptical colleagues that we share common values of learning, discipline, and critical thinking. I have no illusions about the difficulties of these discussions—grading is a controversial topic. But when we focus on principles before practices and on values before policies, we have the opportunity to bring together even the most fractious faculties and communities. FAST grading is, in the end, not just about grading, but about the best practices in teaching and learning.

REFERENCES AND RESOURCES

Alliance for Excellent Education. (Producer). (2015, December 15). *The graduation effect: The economic impact of a high school diploma* [Webinar]. Accessed at http://all4ed.org/webinar-event/dec-15-2015-2 on January 7, 2016.

California Department of Education. (2000). *English–Language Arts Content Standards for California Public Schools: Kindergarten through grade twelve.* Accessed at www.cde.ca.gov/be/st/ss/documents/elacontentstnds.pdf on August 24, 2015.

Chappuis, J., Stiggins, R., Chappuis, S., & Arter, J. (2012). *Classroom assessment for student learning: Doing it right—using it well* (2nd ed.). Boston: Pearson.

DaCosta, M. (Producer and Director). (1962). *The music man* [Motion picture]. United States of America: Warner Brothers.

DuFour, R. (2015). *In praise of American educators: And how they can become even better.* Bloomington, IN: Solution Tree Press.

DuFour, R., DuFour, R., Eaker, R., & Many, T. (2010). *Learning by doing: A handbook for Professional Learning Communities at Work* (2nd ed.). Bloomington, IN: Solution Tree Press.

Elson, L. C. (1909). Story of musical prodigies: How some very remarkable children have afterwards become great musicians and how others have been injured by excessive work in their childhood. *The Etude, 27*(4), 235–236.

Guskey, T. R. (2003). *How's my kid doing? A parent's guide to grades, marks, and report cards.* San Francisco: Jossey-Bass.

Guskey, T. R. (2015). *On your mark: Challenging the conventions of grading and reporting.* Bloomington, IN: Solution Tree Press.

Guskey, T. R., & Bailey, J. M. (2001). *Developing grading and reporting systems for student learning.* Thousand Oaks, CA: Corwin Press.

Hamerman, N. (1993). An early setting of Schiller's "Ode to Joy." *Fidelio* 2(1), 65–66.

Hattie, J. (2009). *Visible learning: A synthesis of over 800 meta-analyses relating to achievement.* London: Routledge.

Hattie, J. (2012). *Visible learning for teachers: Maximizing impact on learning.* London: Routledge.

Hattie, J., & Anderman, E. M. (Eds.). (2013). *International guide to student achievement.* New York: Routledge.

Kohn, A. (2006). *The homework myth: Why our kids get too much of a bad thing.* Cambridge, MA: Da Capo Press.

Kotter, J. P. (1996). *Leading change: An action plan from the world's foremost expert on business leadership.* Boston: Harvard Business School Press.

Marzano, R. J. (2000). *Transforming classroom grading.* Alexandria, VA: Association for Supervision and Curriculum Development.

Marzano, R. J. (2006). *Classroom assessment and grading that work.* Alexandria, VA: Association for Supervision and Curriculum Development.

Marzano, R. J. (2007). *The art and science of teaching: A comprehensive framework for effective instruction.* Alexandria, VA: Association for Supervision and Curriculum Development.

Massachusetts Department of Elementary and Secondary Education. (2015). *National Assessment of Educational Progress. NAEP results.* Accessed at www.doe.mass.edu/mcas/naep/results on January 6, 2016.

National Governors Association Center for Best Practices & Council of Chief State School Officers. (2010). *Common Core State Standards for English language arts and literacy in history/social studies, science, and technical subjects.* Washington, DC: Authors. Accessed at www.corestandards.org/assets/CCSSI_ELA%20Standards.pdf on August 24, 2015.

O'Connor, K. (2007). *A repair kit for grading: Fifteen fixes for broken grades.* Portland, OR: Educational Testing Service.

O'Connor, K. (2011). *A repair kit for grading: Fifteen fixes for broken grades* (2nd ed.). Boston: Pearson.

Pat Summitt Foundation. (n.d.). *Her story.* Accessed at www.patsummitt.org/our_role/pats_story/her_story.aspx on January 5, 2016.

Pérez-Peña, R. (2013, February 1). Students disciplined in Harvard scandal. *The New York Times.* Accessed at www.nytimes.com/2013/02/02 /education/harvard-forced-dozens-to-leave-in-cheating-scandal.html? _r=0 on May 3, 2015.

Quote Investigator. (2012, August 6). It is not enough to succeed; one's best friend must fail [Blog post]. Accessed at www.quoteinvestigator .com/2012/08/06/succeed-fail on March 9, 2016.

Ramírez, E. (2008, December 2). Cheating on the rise among high school students. *U.S. News and World Report* [Blog post]. Accessed at www .usnews.com/education/blogs/on-education/2008/12/02/cheating-on -the-rise-among-high-school-students on May 3, 2015.

Reeves, D. (2005). *Accountability in action: A blueprint for learning organizations* (2nd ed.). Englewood, CO: Advanced Learning Press.

Reeves, D. (2012). The ketchup solution. *American School Board Journal, 189*(7), 35–36.

Reeves, D. (2016). *Elements of grading: A guide to effective practice* (2nd ed.). Bloomington, IN: Solution Tree Press.

Reeves, D. (Ed.) (2007). *Ahead of the curve: The power of assessment to transform teaching and learning.* Bloomington, IN: Solution Tree Press.

Texas Education Agency. (2015). *19 TAC Chapter 110. Texas Essential Knowledge and Skills for English Language Arts and Reading. Subchapter B. Middle School.* Accessed at http://ritter.tea.state.tx.us/rules/tac /chapter110/ch110b.html on January 4, 2016.

Zentall, S. S., & Goldstein, S. (1999). *Seven steps to homework success: A family guide for solving common homework problems.* Plantation, FL: Specialty Press.

INDEX

L

learning
  from failure, 125–127
  peer support for, 129–130
  student learning, expectations for, 45, 61
Levine, J., 126, 131

M

Many, T. W., 12
Marzano, R. J., 2
Massachusetts Institute of technology (MIT), 29–30
mathematical distortions in grading, 77–81
minimum fifty policy, 8–9
Monet, 128
Mozart, W. A., 128
music. *See* arts
Music Man, The, 125

N

National Governors Association (NGA), 11
North High School example, 45–50

O

O'Connor, K., 2, 20
one hundred–point scale, 77

P

parents, getting support from, 28–30
Patterson Elementary School, 40–42
Pedersen, J., 2
peer assessments, 124
peer support for learning, 129–130, 133

Pérez-Peña, R., 115
physical education
  critical thinking, 131–132
  feedback, role of, 127–129
  lessons from failures, 125–127
  peer support for learning, 129–130
  value of, 124–124
pilot projects, 21–22
power standards, 96, 99
preassessments, 7
project-based learning, 77

Q

quiet table, 107

R

Ramírez, E., 115
red–yellow–green system, 106–107
Reeves, D., 1, 2, 76
reflections
  on behavioral issues, 119–120
  on collaboration, 143–145
  on common mistakes, 15
  grading policies examples, 50–52
  on implementing FAST grading, 35–37, 97–100
  on issues for the arts and physical education, 132–134
  on teachers' perspectives on grading, 61–63
  on teachers' time crunch, 108–109
reflective practice, 135
Ross, C., 123, 124

S

Schiller, J.C.F. von, 131

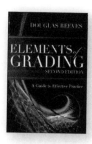

Elements of Grading, Second Edition
Douglas Reeves
The author provides educators with practical suggestions for making the grading process more fair, accurate, specific, and timely. In addition to examples and case studies, new content addresses how the Common Core State Standards and new technologies impact grading practices.
BKF648

On Your Mark
Thomas R. Guskey
Create and sustain a learning environment where students thrive and stakeholders are accurately informed of student progress. Clarify the purpose of grades, craft a vision statement aligned with this purpose, and discover research-based strategies to implement effective grading and reporting practices.
BKF606

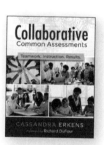

Collaborative Common Assessments
Cassandra Erkens
Reignite the passion and energy assessment practices bring as tools to guide teaching and learning. Strengthen instruction with collaborative common assessments that collect vital information. Explore the practical steps teams must take to establish assessment systems, and discover how to continually improve results.
BKF605

Proficiency-Based Assessment
Troy Gobble, Mark Onuscheck, Anthony R. Reibel, and Eric Twadell
With this resource, teachers will discover how to close the gaps between assessment, curriculum, and instruction by replacing outmoded assessment methods with proficiency-based assessments. Learn the essentials of proficiency-based assessment, and explore evidence-based strategies for successful implementation.
BKF631